What others are saying about Shannon Perry's
Grace in High Heels

"Beautifully weaving together Scripture, personal stories and inspired advice, Shannon Perry speaks to her readers with the compassion and tone of a trusted friend. Her anecdotes elicit laughs and tears, sometimes both on the same page. No matter where you are in your walk with God, there's a message—and a pair of high heels—here for you."

—Kristen Flores, *The Houston Chronicle*

"'Grace in High Heels' is a funny, delight-filled, and soul-refreshing read. It's like having coffee and a good old-fashioned heart-sharing with your best friend!"

—Anita Higman, *best-selling author of*
"Love Finds You in Humble Texas"

"God is using Shannon in a huge way. Anyone who talks to her can tell she cares about people and she is a communicator. Anyone who hears her sing knows she is an incredible talent. For me to share my thoughts on "my sister" is quite the honor. Keep up the amazing work that you do, Shannon. You are the best!"

—Jeff Stice, *2008, 2009, 2010 Singing News Musician*
Of the Year, Founder of the Triumphant Quartet

"I've enjoyed Shannon's gift of music for years, and it's a thrill to hold her devotional in my hand. Her heart for Christ was clear in song and now it is clear in words I can cherish every day."

—DiAnn Mills, *Craftsman Mentor Jerry B. Jenkins*
Christian Writer's Guild, 2010 Christy Award Winner
and best-selling author

"A perfect blend of wit and wisdom, 'Grace in High Heels' offers fresh insights and inspiration to the challenges women face daily!"
> **—Brenda Croucher,** *Women's Ministry Director, Cypress Bible Church*

"As I began to read 'Grace in High Heels,' I got some much- needed laughs from stories like the toilet paper holder entanglement as well as encouragement and entertainment in a "Chick Flick" sort of way. Thank you, Shannon, for your light-hearted stories and wisdom from your heart."
> **—Delia Russell,** *Co-Pastor and Women's Ministry Director, Christ Church Houston Northwest*

"Shannon Perry lives up to the title of her book. If you're looking for real life-faith that's packaged in beauty and style and delivered with grace that abounds, get to know Shannon Perry and her story."
> **—Dr. David Peterson,** *Sr. Pastor, Memorial Drive Presbyterian Church*

"'Grace in High Heels' entrances the reader with 'girl glory' stories and a deeper understanding of God's unending grace. Ready for a taste of extreme faith? This adventure through searing honesty will bring laughter, tears, and a renewed sense of God's humor and over-whelming enchantment with His ladies of all ages."
> **—Bonnie Keen,** *best-selling author and founding member of the award-winning vocal group First Call*

"Having just read, 'Grace in High Heels' I'm ready to reread this delightful, heart-touching tour through life. Within the business arena, there is always a need for the Glory and Wisdom of God. Shannon Perry shares how to walk on HIS path within our own shoes. As a Barbie collector, she was right-on with her comments about Barbie, especially on how to handle our less than Barbie reflection in the mirror. There are lots of people on my 'gift list' who will receive a copy of this inspiration to us all."

–Linda Schmidt, *Shell Employees Federal Credit Union,*
Treasurer & CFO–Retired, Shell Pipe Line Corp./
Shell Oil Co.–Retired, Sharpstown Civic Association, Inc.–VP,
The Down Town Club–Treasurer,
Business & Professional Women, Houston–Treasurer

"From the very moment I met Shannon Perry, there was a feeling of being "soul mates." Her life, teaching and now this wonderful book, reflect the gift of humor that we have been given under that banner of Grace. You will be blessed by her down-to-earth gifts of humor and insight."

–Pat Durham, *Professional Image Coach–Owner,*
Diversity Unlimited

"Shannon writes as she talks, which makes you feel like you've known her all your life. This book will lift your spirits while reassuring you of the one true God who loves you and provides for you in all life's circumstances."

–Gloria Ruppel, *Women's Ministry Director,*
St. Timothy Lutheran Church

"I've often said that when the Grace Train came through town, I was off at Starbucks. Shannon Perry lays it all out for those of us struggling with grace–for ourselves, for our families, for complete strangers–needing a little divine assistance that day. Read this, strap on your high heels, go forth and throw around a little grace. That's what I did."

–Christine Schaub, *critically acclaimed author of*
"Finding Anna" and "The Longing Season"
(Music of the Heart book series)

"Shannon Perry's new book 'Grace in High Heels' is a must read. I found myself laughing one minute and tearing up the next as the truth of God's Word and real life experiences touched my heart. You will be reminded that God's grace is sufficient for everything we go through. Cuddle up in a comfortable chair with this book and get yourself a big dose of God's medicine."

— **Bonnie Cebulak,** *author and Women's Ministry Leader, Missouri*

Grace in High Heels

Grace in High Heels

in

Real-life reflections of humor,
hope and healing

Shannon Perry

Published by Carpenter's Son Publishing, Franklin, TN

Published in association with Larry Carpenter
of Christian Book Services, LLC
www.christianbookservices.com

Cover illustration/design by GKalliance

ISBN-13: 978-0-9849771-7-8

Printed in the United States of America

To order Grace in High Heels, visit the "Store" at www.ShannonPerry.com.

For resources and speaking information, go to www.ShannonPerry.com, or write to Chae Music, P.O. Box 2346, Cypress, TX 77410-2356

Dedicated to my grandmother, Helen Johnson, for her everlasting display of grace.

Grace:

    a.   Unmerited divine assistance given humans for their regeneration or sanctification,

    b.   A virtue coming from God,

    c.   A state of sanctification enjoyed through divine grace.

Acknowledgements

THE Author and Finisher of my faith–thank you, Jesus, for reminding me I always belong with you.

David–thank you for believing in my ability to write and for encouraging me to share it with others. I love you.

Sean–thank you for giving me beautiful content for this book and for being my son. I love you so much.

Mom–your legacy of shoes continues. Thanks for all your encouragement, for taking the time to edit and for traveling many miles with me. I love you.

Dad–thanks for all the days you listened as I ran across the street with yet another idea. Thanks for teaching me to do things with excellence, including the cover of this book. I love you.

Gina Adams–this was your idea! Thanks for the countless hours of input and editing, pushing me to be my best, and making me laugh hysterically along the way.

Laurie Brooks–your tireless efforts helped bring this book to completion. Thank you for editing, formatting and preparing every detail so that *Grace in High Heels* crossed the finish line with excellence.

Lou Hildreth–your encouragement, love and guidance is irreplaceable. Thank you for being a beautiful mentor and real friend.

To my friends who have helped me walk down the paths of this life with courage, determination and a laugh to cover it all, you know who you are—and I love you dearly.

To the ladies who have attended *If the Shoe Fits* events and asked, "Where's your book?" This one's for you!

Table of Contents

Section Three: Lacing Up the Tongue

Section Four: Walk a Mile in My Shoes

Foreword

Whether we are single, married, career women, stay-at-home moms, young, or old, this book is filled with upbeat counsel to bring hope and joy into our lives. Shannon Perry has shared her love for people and her deep faith in God's abundant **grace**. This creative young woman bares her soul with transparent delight, and her stories have us laughing as we identify with her "bad hair" days and other realities of living. Her journeys into a life of obedience and her observations on the power of **grace** are awe-some! Shannon's use of scripture to illustrate these life-lessons is extremely helpful.

A tremendous tool for growth and improvement, "Reflections" at the end of each chapter offers the opportunity to examine ourselves. This incredible book belongs at our fingertips to read, and read again. We can use it daily as encouragement to press on when our lives are in turmoil. We can find the right questions to ask ourselves as we seek to move to higher levels of service. We can learn, laugh, and "grow in the **grace** of our Lord Jesus."

Shannon and I have looked into a television camera, on many occasions, and expressed our desire to tell the world about the **grace** of God. I have listened to her sing her anointed songs and marveled at her teaching skills at conferences where she ministers to multitudes of women. It is my prayer that God will bless all who read this book, and that He will continue to pour out His marvelous **grace** on Shannon Perry, this gifted, chosen minister of the gospel!

Lou Wills Hildreth
Television Host, Gaither Homecoming Artist, Author, Journalist, Member of GMA Hall Of Fame, SGMA Hall Of Fame, Christian Music Hall Of Fame, Texas Gospel Music Hall Of Fame

Prologue

Growing up in a very conservative church, I believed grace was a word that had more to do with walking like a lady than with God's love. As a teenage tomboy, grace was definitely not in my vocabulary. Tripping over my own feet and crashing onto floors was a common occurrence. Playing football with the guys seemed much more appealing than managing hair and makeup. That all changed when I discovered high heels. Unfortunately, balance is required in high heels, and the tomboy in me overshadowed the "Barbie" I wanted to be whenever I wore them.

The lack of grace I exhibited while wearing high heels was a precursor to many life events that would change my view of grace. As I grew older, I realized I no longer needed grace for my shoes—*I needed grace for my life.* I began falling into difficulties instead of down stairs, and tripping over trials instead of my own feet.

Fortunately, God showed me that humor is a powerful tool to help cope with the difficulties we experience. Laughter is both appropriate and required to see the joy in our journey, and I am so grateful for the "real" moments of levity included in this book. Without them, life would have been too somber and lessons may have been lost.

It is my desire to bring practical answers, scriptural truths and contagious humor that will encourage, uplift and free your heart as you read each story.

Each section is designed after the topics in my latest women's conference, *If the Shoe Fits.* The section "Goody Two Shoes" addresses balance and purpose. The stories in "Lacing Up the Tongue" remind us of the importance of our words, and how those words can hurt or heal those we love the most. Stories from "Is There a Hole In Your Sole" teach us that we can overcome any obstacle in our lives and move forward into the plans that God has for us. "Walk a Mile In My Shoes" includes reminders that help us understand what it looks like to live "holy" lives in the "real" world.

At the beginning of each section, you will find words penned during a very difficult season of my life. As I was creating *If the Shoe Fits*, I was also writing songs for a music CD with one of the staff writers from LifeWay Christian Resources in Nashville. These songs were written to enforce the meanings of the topics in *If the Shoe Fits,* and I have included the lyrics to some of these songs at the beginning of each section. Each song was written in hospital waiting rooms as my husband underwent cancer treatment.

My prayer is that you will be "graced" with hope, healing, and humor as you read each chapter, and that you will find the strength to walk in the plans He has designed especially for you.

Section I

Goody Two Shoes

"Remember, Ginger Rogers did everything Fred
Astaire did, but she did it backward
and in high heels."
- Faith Whittlesey -

"Bad Hair Day"

From the CD "The Real Thing"
© 2009 Paul Marino and Shannon Perry

I woke up on the wrong side of the bed
With a laundry list of things to do
running through my head
Right then I should have crawled back in
Cause what came next put me to the test.

The curling iron nearly fried my hair
I dug through the closet,
I couldn't find a thing to wear
Mascara lines all down my face
My heel just broke, and I'm running late.

It's only eight a.m.,
and my brain's already spent
And I'm just a few miles down the road
I spilled coffee on my lap,
as I tried to multi-task
Nothing's going my way
It's a bad hair day!

I pulled in to the Wal-Mart parking lot
Some pretty little trophy princess
tries to steal my spot
My check-out clerk is newly hired
I can't find my cash, and my card's expired

And now it's three p.m.,
and my nerves are wearing thin
Doing the car pool after school
I started heading down the street
with the wrong kids in my backseat
Oh what more can I say,
it's a bad hair day!

I broke a nail, dog with fleas,
credit cards with hidden fees
It's enough to drive a girl insane
Soccer, basketball and dance,
piano lessons start again
Mortgage due, homework's late
Will I ever get a break?

It's finally six p.m.,
and I'm at my wit's end
The dinner's burned again tonight
The laundry's piled up high
My phone's dead and so am I
Nothing more I can say
It's a bad hair day!

CHAPTER ONE

Learning to Praise on Bad Hair Days

"In all this you greatly rejoice, though now for a little while you may have had to suffer grief in all kinds of trials. These have come so that the proven genuineness of your faith—of greater worth than gold, which perishes even though refined by fire—may result in praise, glory and honor when Jesus Christ is revealed."
1 Peter 1: 6-7 (NIV)

Have you ever had a "bad hair" day? I am not referring to the kind that the curling iron can cure, but to those days when events in your life seem unbelievable.

It was Sunday and I was running late for a concert. I was due for a sound check in thirty minutes and the church was forty-five minutes from my home. I was fifteen minutes into my commute when I realized I had forgotten a significant piece of music that I needed for the event. A friend of mine had a copy nearby, so I called him and quickly drove to his office. As I jumped out of my car in a panic, I quickly shut the door. *You guessed it!* My keys were hanging from the ignition and all of the doors were locked.

Not only was I certain to miss the sound check, it would be a miracle if I made the concert.

My friend called a wrecker to get the keys out of my car while I called the church to let them know about my delay. Forty-five minutes later, the wrecker driver arrived with a "Slim Jim" in hand. As he worked on one side of the car, my friend walked around to the other side. With a loud shout of disbelief, he suddenly screamed, "Shannon!" He then put his hand through the window that was down on the other side of the car. *My first reaction was shock, and then I laughed uncontrollably.* The wrecker driver shook his head in disbelief, and refused to take payment for his visit. I quickly thanked my friend, apologized for any inconvenience, and jumped into my car. I arrived at the church in time for the concert, and the congregation enjoyed a great laugh as I explained my delay.

How many times have you felt locked out of solutions that you need for your life? Maybe the opposite is true. Maybe you feel locked inside of a situation that seems hopeless and you need a wrecker driver to get you out. I have learned that *Jesus is the ultimate deliverer.* There are two men in the Bible who certainly found this to be true as well.

In Acts 16, Paul and Silas were definitely having what most of us would consider a **very** "bad hair" day. Beaten and unjustly thrown into prison for worshipping the living God, Paul and Silas were placed in chains and under very tight security. Instead of complaining, however, they began singing praises to

God while sitting in their chains.

Praises in prison? I don't know about you, but it is often difficult for me to get over myself and sing praises to God when I am having a "bad hair" day, much less when I am treated unfairly. These men knew the secret to overcoming difficulties. They took their eyes off their circumstances, and put them completely on to God.

As they were singing in their cell, an earthquake came and the prison doors were opened. Although they could have immediately escaped, they chose to stay where they were. Because of their example of faith, the jailer and his family gave their lives to Christ.

Maybe you need an earthquake today. You have found yourself in a prison, and you don't know how to sing praises on your "bad hair" days. Your prison may not seem significant to others, but it weighs you down and keeps you from God's best. How can we receive our "earthquake?" How can we have victory during our "bad hair" days? The same way that Paul and Silas did. They found the key to their prison doors through praise.

Praise is the prayer that changes everything.

Praise keeps our minds on Christ and off our circumstances. Praise releases the power of God to work in our circumstances. Whether our prison is created by injustice or by our own hands, God longs for us to live a life of freedom in Him.

When "bad hair" days come and you hear the slam of

the prison door, begin to thank God that He knows the way out. We can take refuge in the One who still opens prison doors and sets captives free. As a result, our victories become encouraging to others and our "bad hair" days become great days of praise.

Reflection

1. What is your reaction on "bad hair" days? Can you identify with Paul and Silas as you praise your way through the situation?

2. How can you keep your focus on Christ when circumstances shake your foundation?

3. What are some ways that you praise?

CHAPTER TWO

Raggedy Ann in a Barbie Doll World

"But I am like an olive tree flourishing in the house of God; I trust in God's unfailing love for ever and ever."
Psalm 52:8 (NIV)

Do you feel like Raggedy Ann living in a Barbie doll world? This question caught my attention recently while shopping with friends at a Louisiana craft store. It also made me laugh hysterically. Why? *Because I could identify!*

As I speak and sing at women's conferences throughout the country, I have many opportunities to talk with women who also feel like Raggedy Ann, or "Annie" as I like to call her. They have had the life squeezed from them, but feel obligated to meet life's demands looking like Barbie.

On my drive home from Louisiana to Texas, I began thinking about Barbie and Annie. I found some interesting comparisons. Annie's hair is usually all over the place; Barbie's hair is perfectly in place. Annie wears an apron; Barbie wears an evening gown. Annie wears no shoes; Barbie wears stilettos.

And that's when it hit me! We often see ourselves as

lifeless Raggedy Ann dolls, while God sees us as beautiful Barbies.

"For God sees not as man sees, for man looks at the outward appearance, but the Lord looks at the heart."
I Samuel 16:7 (NASB)

While media and magazines push outward extravagance, God longs for our hearts to worship Him extravagantly.

Don't get me wrong ladies. Every barn looks better with a little paint! There is nothing wrong with looking good, but our focus must be *balanced*. So, how do we accomplish our Annie tasks while taking care of ourselves like Barbie?

The first thing to remember when balancing our lives is that *we cannot do it all.* We put a lot of pressure on ourselves to be everything to everyone. This often happens when we fear something is lacking, so we wear ourselves out trying to fill the void. We must protect our priorities and relinquish the things that steal our time. For example, enjoy time with your children, even if the house is not perfect. Strive to keep an orderly home, but know that your children will remember the quality time you spend with them much more than the dirty dishes that were left in the sink.

We need to *take care of ourselves.* There is a balanced way to do this, and we must care for ourselves if we are going to care for others. Be sure to rest, eat well, exercise and do something you enjoy while maintaining the responsibilities that God has given you. It is rare that anyone needs us 24 hours a day. Make a decision that you will take care of yourself so that you can care for others with excellence.

Finally, stop focusing on what is wrong with you, and *take an inventory of what you do right!* As women, we often find it easy to name our flaws while struggling to list our strengths. If this is difficult for you, write down five things you do right each day. Make a conscious decision to examine the good qualities about yourself, and focus on those things as you continue to make progress in the other areas.

Continue to focus on the good things! You are a beautiful Barbie in the eyes of your Heavenly Father.

Reflection

1. What areas of your life need more balance?

2. How will you accomplish balance in each of these areas?

3. What scriptures do you repeat to yourself as a reminder of the way God sees you?

4. What things do you need to relinquish to Him today?

CHAPTER THREE

Planes, Strings and Toilet Paper Rolls

"But to each one of us grace has been given as Christ apportioned it." Ephesians 4:7 (NIV)

My mom and I have shared many special moments throughout the years. Several of those memories have been made as we travel to women's events where I minister. While my mom fondly remembers days of tearooms and trellises, a favorite memory of mine occurred in the Nashville airport.

Mom and I were preparing to board a plane headed back to Houston from Nashville, and I decided to go to the restroom before we left. My mom quickly reminded me that I would not have time because we were due for boarding any minute and the restroom was two gates down from ours. I found this rather humorous, knowing that no matter how old I get, my mom continues to monitor my bathroom breaks. *Promising to return quickly*, I jumped from my seat and headed down the terminal.

Upon finishing my business in the restroom, I reached for the toilet paper and found myself in a most peculiar position. Unbeknownst to me, as I had been unwrapping the toilet paper from the roll, the long strings of my sweatshirt hoodie had mysteriously become entangled in the toilet paper holder. The more I tried to free myself, the tighter I was bound to the toilet paper roll. With my head now glued to the wall above the paper holder, I did what any 40-something-year-old would do. From that stall in the airport bathroom, I began yelling at the top of my lungs, "MOM! MOM! MUHHH-THERRRRRR!"

Amazingly, no matter how old a child grows, a mother instinctively hears their cry. This episode was no exception. With the speed of Superwoman, my mom sprinted past two gates, burst into the bathroom and screamed, "WHAT IS THE MATTER WITH YOU?" *"I am hung in the toilet paper roll holder,"* I cried. With a pause that seemed to last for eternity, she managed to utter her only word, "WHAT?" *"You heard me,"* I quickly retorted. "The strings of my shirt are wound up in the toilet paper roll holder and I cannot get loose." "Well, just open the door," my mother suggested.

Obviously, she did not realize the tug of war that had ensued inside that stall. The toilet paper roll holder had won, and I could not move forward, backward or sideways. I certainly could not reach the door! At this point, I could only imagine the janitors finding us at midnight as they put out their "Wet Floor" signs. The only alternative was for my mother to crawl under the door of the stall.

With the determination of a bull, my mother, the epitome of a Southern Bell, kicked off her heels, hiked up her skirt and started under the bathroom door. After what seemed like hours of wiggling and squeezing, she completed her mission and met me face to face with a warning unlike any I had heard from her before: "Don't you *EVER* do this again!" We stared at each other in disbelief, and then began to laugh uncontrollably. After freeing me from the toilet paper holder, we quickly made our way back to the gate and caught our flight just in time for our trip home.

As women, we have many things to balance in our lives. At times, we get into situations that are awkward to say the least because we take on too much. We find ourselves struggling to find a starting place because we don't know how to say, "No." Then we get mad at the ones we said, "Yes" to because we don't really want to do what we said we would do. This trap can cause us to hurt ourselves, our relationships with others, and even with God. How? Because *God will only give us the grace to do what He has called us to do.*

When we become frustrated and "stuck," we need to stop and ask God about our part. If we are taking on too much, we need to find out where He would have us cut back, then do it. We will be a lot happier in the long run and much more pleasant to be around. We will also avoid some very awkward situations that keep us "wrapped" up in things much worse than toilet paper holders!

Reflection

1. What are some awkward situations you have found yourself in because you could not say, "No"?

2. What are some moments where you said, "No" and felt confident about your decision?

3. What part does God's will play in your decision to say, "Yes" or "No"? How can you keep His will at the center of your decisions?

CHAPTER FOUR

Put It Down!

"Let me be weighed in an even balance, that God may know my integrity." Job 31:6 (ASV)

It was early April and I was attending a girl-friend's wedding shower with many of my colleagues. I must tell you that short of wallpapering, showers are not a high priority on my "to do" list. I love the food and socializing, but passing around the gifts has become somewhat of an intimidating experience for me. I find myself running out of adjectives and there are only so many ways to say, "Isn't that cute," or "Isn't that nice?" I am usually thinking ONE thing:

"When are we going to eat?"

I often find that we conduct ourselves quite different-ly at showers than the way we do at home. At showers we walk daintily with one finger in the air as we carry our punch glass. At home, however, we take the coke can from the refrigerator and slam the contents down our throat in one sip. I tend to do the latter. At this shower I did my best dainty impression and was *thrilled* when the hostess announced that it was time to eat.

I marveled at the sandwiches, chips, cake and nuts on the table. I carefully filled my plate and thought to myself, *"This shower either has undersized plates or oversized food."* My plate was quickly filled so I carefully stepped toward the punchbowl. As I reached for the ladle, I realized I had nowhere to sit my plate because the table was completely covered with food. I began to panic. How did they expect me to do all of this with one hand?

I looked across the table to see a lady gracefully maneuver her plate and cup in the same hand. As she held her plate and punch cup with her left hand, she smoothly filled her cup with the ladle in her right. I shifted my cup to my left hand and followed suit. I was so proud of my new found coordination until I noticed there were elements in the punch bowl that had NOT been there before: chips… a cookie… a sandwich? Just what kind of surprises did this hostess have in mind? *Then I realized those were MY surprises!* As I was filling my punch cup, I had also filled the punchbowl with every item on my plate!

Had anyone seen what I had done? Maybe I could just walk away from the table and it would be a mystery. Many methods of escape rushed through my mind until my dear friend behind me announced to all in attendance, *"Well, you can take the girl out of the country, but you can't take the country out of the girl!"* I wanted to dive under the table! I was no longer the dainty shower attendee I had hoped to be. I felt more like the homecoming queen whose heel is caught in the turf of the football field as her title is announced. *I was caught!*

I smiled nervously as the hostess approached me. Her lips appeared to move in slow motion as I anticipated her response. My pulse slowed and my face relaxed as she graciously announced, "Don't worry. We have plenty of punch." She picked up the bowl and proceeded to fill it with fresh punch.

Needless to say, I am still somewhat skeptical of showers, but I have learned my lesson. If your hands are too full, **put something down!**

There are great similarities between this shower and our lives. When we try to hold too much in our hands, we get out of balance, and we often make a mess as a result. The good news is that we have a Heavenly Father who treats us the same way the hostess treated me. *He graciously comes behind us, cleans up our mess, and gives us a fresh start.*

When you find yourself out of balance, ask God if there is something that you need to put down. God does not call us to do it all. His grace, combined with the gifts and talents He has given us, will help us accomplish all that we need to do. The next time you feel like your hands are too full, *ask the Holy Spirit to refill your cup with only those things that He has planned for you.* After all, He is the perfect host of this party called "Life."

Reflection

1. In what areas of your life is your plate over-flowing? Are there some things that you need to put down today?

2. Are you making excuses for holding on to some things that God is calling you to put down? How will your obedience affect your walk with Christ?

3. How have you seen God graciously come behind you and clean up after a mess in your life?

CHAPTER FIVE

Who's the Boss?

"Train up a child in the way he should go, and when he is old he will not depart from it." Proverbs 22:6 (NKJV)

I am often asked if I miss my days of being a schoolteacher and school counselor. Without a doubt, my response is, "Yes!" But do you know what I miss? I miss listening to kids and watching them. Even as I write this, I am in a public place where children are continually passing in front of me and I can hear their conversations. One teenager skipped by singing, "Mom is gonna get you, Mom is gonna get you!" as her brother lagged four steps behind. Another little boy was yelling, "Dad, I LOVE sugar," and a little girl with pink bows in her hair asked, "Mom, do you think I am pretty?" *Kids are great!* What would we do without their innocent smiles and naive ways of thinking?

In our fast paced world, we have become a society of instant everything. Unfortunately, this often includes our relationship with our kids. We expect quick answers when we are at work, so we give our kids quick answers when they question us. We live in a world of convenience, so we become easily irritated when our kids don't cooperate with our agenda. We have everything available at the touch of a button, so our patience is limited. Drive-through dinners are at an all-time high and dinnertime with family is slowly becoming a thing of the past. Yet we wonder what is happening to our kids? It is not complicated. Many are learning how to live by following the examples that surround them. *Scary, isn't it?*

I haven't been a mom for long, but I have been one long enough to make some significant mistakes. Like the time I told Sean he could have friends over to spend the night. I certainly didn't realize that those "friends" also included friends of the opposite sex. This particular group had been friends for so long that they didn't think anything of it. *I certainly did!* David and I had just gotten married and I really wanted Sean to "like" me so I said, "Yes." The girls had to stay upstairs and the boys had to stay downstairs. They honored my request, but I was a nervous wreck all night. I conveniently had a cough every thirty minutes and got water in the kitchen as I walked the house like a Drill Sargent. It would have been much easier, and I could have gotten some sleep, if I would have just said that one little word… "No!"

One truth I have learned as a teacher, counselor and teen conference speaker is this: *children are begging for boundaries.* Need some proof? Just look at the newspaper, television or juvenile detention centers. Watch the youth group at your church or observe some conversations on Facebook. Children want to know there are limits. Why? It makes them feel safe.

Just as we enjoy knowing that there are boundaries around our homes, kids enjoy knowing that there are boundaries around their lives. Boundaries take time to establish and following through is where it gets tough. We have busy lives and taking the time to establish boundaries often takes away from our other priorities. Here is the great part: *When we take time to set boundaries, it saves us a lot of hurt, heartache and frustration in the future.*

During my years as a counselor, one of the more horrifying stories I remember came from the mom of a preschooler. Sitting in my office, she elaborated through unending tears about the struggles she was having at home. She went on to tell me how her preschool daughter was running everyone in the house, and they could not get her under control. As you might imagine, this mother and I had a long discussion, but it didn't take long to identify the problem. *Mom was afraid to set healthy boundaries* and as a result, a four-year-old was running her life!

God's Word gives us great examples of leaders who experienced boundaries. King David certainly understood God's stand on boundaries. Read the book of Psalms. Remember Moses? The book of Exodus is filled with stories of God's boundaries and the people's response to such limits.

There are three areas that you may want to keep in mind when setting boundaries with your kids. First, make sure that the boundaries are *age appropriate.*

Do not allow your twelve-year-old unlimited access to the Internet. Second, make sure the boundaries are *realistic*. As our children grow, so does their need for more independence. Use the boundaries to teach them healthy ways of becoming more independent. And third, *reinforce* the boundaries you set. At some point, you will face opposition. That is the worst time to give up or change the boundary. If you feel that the boundary is truly unfair, wait until the difficulty has passed, then sit down with your child and discuss why you are changing it. If you change it when they throw a tantrum or get mad, you have taught them that they can manipulate you.

Parenting is never easy. We may not always get it right, but we can rest assured that God will help us each step of the way when we parent with His ideas in mind.

Reflection

1. Are there any new boundaries that you need to set with your child? What is a healthy way to do so?

2. Do you need to analyze some of the boundaries that you currently have in place? Are there any boundaries that need to be more strictly reinforced? Are there any that need to be changed?

3. What are some boundaries that God has put in place for your life? How do you respond to those boundaries?

CHAPTER SIX

All But One

"For though I am absent from you in body, I am present with you in spirit and delight to see how orderly you are and how firm your faith is in Christ." Colossians 2:5 (NIV)

There is a high priority placed on organizational skills these days. Just visit any bookstore and it won't take long to find books titled, "Getting it Together," and "Freedom to Live the Clutter Free Life."

For years, I have worked on getting my life organized. Unfortunately, my efforts usually last until the next set of demands and schedule changes. Soon my life is back to its unorganized state. One experience that taught me a significant lesson about order came when I was much younger.

When I was in eighth grade, I went on a mission trip to Mexico with the youth group from my church. After teaching a wonderful Bible school that week and seeing many children give their lives to Christ, it was time to return to Houston. Our youth director instructed us to pack our suitcases and set them at the end of our beds for our departure the following morning. Everyone did as they were told. Everyone but me, that is. I had connected with some friends from another church who were also staying at the campsite and I wanted to go to their Friday night church service. My youth director granted me special permission to stay out late so I enjoyed our last evening in Mexico with new friends while the others turned in early.

At midnight, I returned to our cabin. All of the girl's suitcases were neatly packed at the end of their bunks. My belongings, on the other hand, were strewn across my bed. At thirteen years old, I was more worried about sleep than organization so I shoved my clothes onto the floor and crawled under the sheet.

During the middle of the night, one of the girls in my room woke up screaming. Thinking she might be having night terrors, our counselor turned on the lights. Suddenly, more than that one girl was screaming. All fifty girls were screaming. While we were all sleeping, someone had come through an open window of our cabin and stolen every suitcase. *All but one, that is.* Since my things were still on the floor, the intruder gave up on my bunk and I was the only one left with any of my belongings. Police later determined that a truck full of men backed up to the cabin in the middle of the night and walked through our dorm as we lay sleeping. They weren't interested in taking any of us, but they got all of the suitcases... *all but one.*

Life has a way of changing us, so I have certainly tried to become more orderly in my later years. I am married to a man who knows when a pencil is out of place, so the Perry home is usually very tidy. So why is order such an important part of our lives? I think it all goes back to the beginning…

When God took nothing and made it into something, He was creating a sense of order. He was creating a sense of *purpose.*

I am shocked when I ask women at a conference, "How many of you know your purpose?" Less than twenty percent usually raise their hands. TWENTY PERCENT! This tells me that nearly eighty percent of women in the world *simply exist* and they don't even know why. So many of us get into a rut that we don't even think about *why* we are doing what we are doing anymore… *we just do it.*

If we are to live a life of order, then we must follow God's plan. His plan includes *purpose.* There is always a purpose for the things that He does and He left us a great example to follow through His Word. Remember the flood? Know anyone that could have gotten all those animals to actually walk into that Ark without order and purpose? Or how about the Red Sea? Haven't seen that one happen before or since.

God does things with purpose, and so should we.

How about you? Are you walking with purpose today or are you going through life *just getting by*? Today, I challenge you to get on your face before God and ask Him to show you if you are where **He** wants you to be. Chances are good that you already know if you are walking in your purpose. If you are not and you would like to know your purpose, there is an easy way to find out… ASK!

"If any of you lacks wisdom, he should ask God, who gives generously to all without finding fault, and it will be given to him." James 1:5 (NIV)

When we ask with right motive, which is to bring Honor to God with our lives, He will answer. He will take even the most mundane life and give it great purpose!

Ask yourself some questions today. "Am I fitting into God's plan? What do I long to do with my life? What gifts and talents has God given me so that I can accomplish His plan? What do I need to do to begin moving forward to serve God in the plan that He has designed especially for me?"

Are you looking for order in your life today? *Start with your purpose.* Ask God to show you HIS purpose for this season of your life. Remind Him that you know He is a God of order and that to feel His order in your life, you want to know His purpose for you. Once He tells you, GET MOVING! If you have been focused on a different area and God tells you to move, DO IT! What may seem the appropriate sense of order in your life may not be what God is saying to you at all.

If you think you have gone too far today and there is no turning back, remember my story. Just like my suitcase, God can take our mess and make something good come from it. Things may seem like a MESS on the surface, but the same God who parted the Red Sea and got the animals to the Ark is ready to walk you into the destiny *He has purposed… just for you!*

Reflection

1. Identify the gifts and talents that God has given you. If you do not know what they are, ask others around you who know you well and will be honest with you.

2. Ask God to show you what He would like to do with the gifts and talents He has given to you. When you pray, surrender to His purpose for your life.

3. Journal each day and take note of each time you do things that include your gifts and talents. Then pray, and ask God to continue guiding you through the doors He opens for you and closing those that are not intended for you.

SHANNON PERRY

CHAPTER SEVEN

Let Go of the Trigger

"He changes times and seasons; He removes kings and sets up kings; He gives wisdom to the wise and knowledge to those who have understanding." Daniel 2:21 (NKJV)

Don't you love when the seasons change? Colored leaves cover the trees in the fall and life is reborn in the spring. Just as the weather changes with each passing season, so do events we experience in the seasons of our lives. Change can be frightening, but new events are an amazing opportunity to see God move on our behalf.

Recently, I elected to try something new when my husband and I had a large delivery of dirt brought to our home. Unfortunately, the trucks left as much dirt on the driveway as they did on our grass. Determined to do my husband a favor, I decided to try my hand at power washing the driveway.

After rolling the washer onto the driveway, I stared at it for a moment. *Couldn't I just plug this thing in and it would start?* With modern technology, the idea of pulling a cord seemed absurd. I rolled up my sleeves, placed my foot against the washer, and began pulling. Each time I pulled the cord, the washer would roll away from me. After **fifteen minutes** of striving to start this contraption, I finally found the choke. The designer of this machine was *brilliant!* He knew that "choking" the machine was **exactly** what I felt like doing after multiple failed attempts.

With one pull of the choke, the washer started. Unfortunately, so did the wand I was holding which sprays the water and I quickly began spinning around the driveway like a deflated balloon. I bounced from one side of the driveway to another as the force of the water spun me in circles like a top. I was soaking wet and laughing hysterically once I realized the source of my malfunction: LET GO OF THE TRIGGER!

Is your finger "glued" to the trigger today? Is there anything you need to let go of in this season of your life?

"There is a time for everything, and a season for every activity under Heaven." Ecclesiastes 3:1 (NIV)

Maybe you are in the infancy of *spring* where new ideas and situations are exciting, but the work to get them done is overwhelming. Let go of anxiety, and trust God with the details.

Perhaps you are in the stability of *summer* where you have accomplished great things in your family, work and ministry, but they must be maintained. Let go of any lies that whisper "there is something better, and the grass is always greener." Thank God for bringing you to this place, and ask Him to help you maintain those *"good and perfect gifts"* that He has given you. (James 1:17 NIV)

Are you in the *fall* season of life where change is inevitable? Let go of the fear of change and remember the promise of God's Word.

"Jesus Christ is the same, yesterday, today, and forever." Hebrews 13:8 (NIV)

No matter what changes we are facing, God is able and He **never** changes.

If you are in the *winter* of your life, things may seem frozen, where nothing is able to grow. Remember the changes that occur in vegetation during the winter season. The seed does not move and may in fact have no activity. While the seed certainly looks dead, new birth is taking place in the stillness of the winter months.

"He will not let your foot slip—He who watches over you will not slumber..." Psalm 121:3 (NIV)

His faithfulness is consistent in **all** seasons. As you sit still during this winter season, amazing rebirth is taking shape in your life.

Whatever season you are in; remember that the changing of seasons is inevitable. Don't let life spin you around uncontrollably like that power washer on the driveway. LET GO OF THE TRIGGER. Allow God to *wash away* whatever needs to be cleaned up so that this season brings about His perfect plan for your life.

"My power is made perfect in weakness."
2 Corinthians 12:9 (NIV)

When we pray, we approach the power that is able to do exceedingly above all that we ask in every season of our life. Trust Him, and know you are loved during this season, *and always.*

Reflection

1. What season of life are you currently in? What are you asking God to do through this season?

2. Is there anything currently spinning you out of control? What scripture are you clinging to as you hold onto God's promises during this time?

3. Is there a situation in your life where you need to take your hand off the trigger and allow God to move in and work?

Section II

Is There a Hole in

Your Sole?

"If God sends us on strong paths,
we are provided strong shoes."
- *Corrie TenBoom* -

"Keep On Pressing On"

From the CD "The Real Thing"
© 2009 Paul Marino and Shannon Perry

Life seldom turns out the way you plan it
In one blink of an eye, everything can fall apart
And all of the things that you simply
    take for granted
Vanish in the night,
    and make you wonder why?

When the going gets tough,
keep on pressing on
When the road is rough,
keep on moving on
With each step along the way,
He will be your strength
You're not alone,
He'll lead you home
Keep on pressing on.

There is a cross that is waiting for the broken
And all who will come, His forgiveness is there
All of the past was overcome
    when it was spoken,
"It is done, it is done."

When the going gets tough,
keep on pressing on
When the road is rough,
keep on moving on
With each step along the way,

He will be your strength
You're not alone,
He'll lead you home
Keep on pressing on.

When you've had enough,
He will hold you up.

When the going gets tough,
keep on pressing on
When the road is rough,
keep on moving on
With each step along the way,
He will be your strength
You're not alone,
He'll lead you home
Keep on pressing on.

CHAPTER EIGHT

Power in the Holes

"God is not a man that He should lie, nor a son of man that He should change His mind. Does He speak and then not act? Does He promise and not fulfill?" Numbers 23:19 (NIV)

As I speak and sing at women's events around the country, I am amazed at some of the practical lessons God continues to give me while teaching His Word. One such lesson happened on stage.

While teaching the topic "Is There a Hole In Your Sole?" from my latest conference series **If the Shoe Fits** I was reminding the women how we often get stuck in emotional holes, when suddenly, *I was stuck.* Not in an emotional hole, but in the hole of an electrical outlet. The door to an electrical outlet on the stage had been left open and the stiletto heel I was wearing was wedged in the opening. I tried to walk forward, but was unsuccessful. Determined to free myself, I rocked slowly back and forth. I later learned that some of the women thought I was either having a seizure or feeling a tremendous move of the Spirit. Unable to free myself, I finally told the audience I was stuck, bent over and with a huge tug, removed my shoe from the opening. As the women laughed hysterically, I smiled gracefully, slid the shoe back on my foot, and continued our lesson on holes.

Have you ever been stuck in a hole? Not like the one on the stage, but an emotional hole that won't seem to heal? Maybe your hole is divorce, or the loss of a child, or abuse, or addiction, or depression? Whatever your hole, rest assured that Jesus did not stay "stuck" in the hole that was created for him on the day of his death. When Jesus died, Satan must have thought he had won the greatest battle in history. With his vile and deceitful tongue, he whispered, "You are defeated Jesus, and I am the winner."

How many times has Satan deceived you into thinking that you have been defeated? Have you learned to live in the hole, or are you trusting that the same power that raised Jesus from the dead is able to resurrect you from the holes in your life? Psalm 40:1-3 is a powerful reminder of what God will do when we put our trust in Him. He will lift us from the pit, and give us a new song.

There is nothing that can heal a hole in our soul but the Living God. People, jobs, status, money, houses, dreams, and all of the other answers that the world offers are powerless to heal the deepest places in our soul. Unfortunately, we live in a world where we are often told that WE hold the keys to our answers. The only One who holds the keys to the answers, however,

paid the ultimate price when He gave His life on the

cross.

As Jesus hung on the cross, He was well acquainted with holes. Holes in his hands held Him to the cross; one He loved inflicted a hole in his side. Holes were pierced through His feet, the same feet that willingly walked to their death. The holes in His head came from a crown that publicly mocked Him. The hole in his heart, however, was the greatest and the one that Satan believed was the final blow. *The next hole, however, would change everything.*

When Jesus' body was placed in a borrowed "hole" for three days, the power of any circumstance that we will ever experience was overcome. Satan was defeated when Jesus came bursting through that hole on the third day after His death, and nothing will ever reverse that victory. WE WIN!

Today, do your holes seem incurable? Perhaps Satan has whispered the same lie to you that he did to Jesus, "You are defeated."

Jesus longs for us to walk in the power of what He did for us on the cross. He died so that we could have eternal life, but He also died so that we could walk in the freedom that came by His blood. Because we are the beneficiaries of the inheritance of the cross, you and I can know overcoming power and victory on a daily basis when we put all of our trust in Him.

If you are like me, I find that most holes do not disappear overnight. *It is a process.* So what can we do in the process to help heal the holes in our soul? First, *trust God* and Him only. Secondly, *cry out* to God for healing. Psalm 72:12 reminds us that *"He will deliver the needy who cry out…"* *(NIV)* And finally, *press on*. When the Father of lies whispers, "You are finished," remind him of the everlasting promise that you received from the cross, "It is finished."

Reflection

1. Are there "holes" in your sole that you long for God to heal? Identify them and ask God to show you His healing in each area.

2. What are some of the lies that keep you from believing you are victorious over the holes in your life?

3. Find a source of Scripture that will encourage you the next time you feel defeated. Quote that scripture out loud as a powerful reminder that YOU WIN!

CHAPTER NINE

The Ride

"Tell the righteous it will be well with them, for they will enjoy the fruit of their deeds." Isaiah 3:10 (NIV)

Sometimes things just don't work out according to plan. This is not just a suggestion from a line in one of my songs. *It is the truth.*

So how do we deal with the really big disappointments in life? Allow me to tell you about one of the greatest and most Godly women I have ever known. Introducing... my grandmother.

My grandmother and grandfather were married for forty-eight years. They raised their family in church, and made sure that their children and grandchildren knew Jesus.

Shortly after their forty-eighth anniversary, my grandfather retired from the steel plant and my grandmother would soon retire from her position of forty years as the Children's Director at their church. They had always talked about doing **one** thing after retirement... *traveling.* Their dream was to visit places that they had always wanted to see, so after my grandmother's retirement, they would hit the road.

That's when things hit the fan...

My grandfather began spending more and more time away from home and more and more time on the phone. When my grandmother would ask him to talk, he had nothing to say. Before long, our suspicions were confirmed. While my grandmother was working at church, Satan was working in our family. My grandfather became involved with another woman and announced to our family that he was divorcing my grandmother.

We were all devastated. We did everything that we knew to do and prayed every prayer that we knew to pray. My grandmother cried and we cried with her. *It was all to no avail.* Once someone has their mind made up, even God will not force His will on them. He will intervene on our behalf.

My grandfather soon married his mistress so my grandmother decided that she could begin again. *I must tell you,* if I ever get to a place where I feel like giving up, I think of her. She was the ultimate picture of determination. She prayed for God's help, asked Him to take her brokenness and decided she would travel-with or without my grandfather.

Now my grandmother had rarely been out of East Texas, much less out of the state of Texas. Every time the Senior Citizen trips rolled around however, she packed her suitcase and got on the bus. She later told me that sometimes, she didn't even know where they were going, and quite frankly, she didn't care. God was allowing her to do what she had always wanted to do. Her life was playing out differently than she had planned, but *she trusted God and she traveled on.*

She shared one trip that is **forever** etched in the minds of my family. While in California, her senior group took a trip to Disneyland. While she was not one for riding a great deal of rides, she said she spotted one that looked fairly calm, so she decided to try it. It was the "ET" ride. She said they had cute little bikes so she thought she would settle in for a nice bike ride through the park. Little did she know that the "ET" ride was a ROLLER COASTER! My grandmother and all the other eighty-year-olds boarded the ride and prepared for their "bike ride." At first, the ride is slow and takes you through the "ET" movie set. After that, the cars suddenly drop 50 feet and the rest of the ride is crazy!

My grandmother said all she remembers is seeing "ET's" head bobbing back and forth in the basket on her "handle bars" and the old lady next to her saying, *"I am going to die Helen. I am going to die right here."* After making it safely off the ride, my grandmother opted to sit and eat ice cream for the rest of her stay at Disneyland.

Have you ever thought that you were going on a *leisurely* bike ride only to find yourself on a roller coaster? It may not have been at Disneyland but life took you for a ride that you weren't expecting. Maybe it wasn't the betrayal of a spouse, but it was the death of a child, or the loss of a job or the betrayal of a friend. Whatever your rollercoaster ride, it was not expected and you had to *hang on for dear life until the ride was over.*

So what do we do when we are in those unexpected places? I learned from watching my Grandmother. First, we **pray**. We pray every day, every hour, and sometimes, every second. Then, we **surrender**. We surrender all of our feelings, hopes, wants, dreams and plans to the One who can take our lives and put them back together when they have been destroyed. Next, we **trust**. We believe God's Word is sovereign and that He can do exactly what He says He will do for us. Then, we **live**.

When we have been in the valley of despair, climbing out is sometimes hard. We want to avoid others, disengage and hide. While this may be good for a season, it is not healthy long term. The Bible reminds us to *"forsake not the assembling of ourselves together." (Hebrews 10:25 NKJV)* Why? Because we find strength and hope as we see God working in the lives of others.

What about our feelings of injustice? When we find ourselves on the roller coaster, we often wonder why the one who flipped the switch did not have to take the ride? In other words, *why did the one who caused the hurt seem to get off scot-free?* I wish I had a better answer for you but the best explanation I have heard is this: God is our vindicator, and He will decide who needs vindicating and in what time frame. If we sit around worrying about what our offender is doing, or how God is going to get him/her, we allow that person to control our lives. *God is fully aware of the situation* and much more capable of handling it than we will ever be. What happens to us may be far from fair, but God knows when to move and what to do and he doesn't need our help.

When we are broken, God is able to pick up the pieces and make us a beautiful person who is able to reflect His light. *Take stained glass for example.* When light hits a stained glass picture it reflects light in a thousand different directions because of the broken pieces of glass the picture contains. One of those pieces of glass would not be nearly as beautiful by itself and they certainly wouldn't reflect light unless they were broken. This is where the difference comes. Many choose to hold onto their brokenness and become bitter and angry. They do not allow God to do what He does best–take the broken pieces and make them into something beautiful. As a result, their hearts grow cold and ugly. Then, they are even unhappier and for the rest of their lives, they blame the one who "broke" them. That, my sweet friend, is called a victim. Yes, we have been hurt, yes we have been wronged and yes it was unfair. But what does holding on to the anger and resentment bring except sickness and death? Those aren't my words; those are God's   words. *"Do not let the sun go down on your wrath." (Ephe-*

sians 4:26 NKJV) Why? Because He knows the damage that anger and resentment do to us.

So what is the alternative? *Give God the broken pieces.* Kicking, screaming, and crying all the way, tell Him you are determined to make it and to come through this trial with His help. Your plans may have been severely altered, but let Him know you trust Him, then, surrender. Remember, "YOU can't, HE can, let HIM."

My grandmother certainly did. She continued working and taking trips but she never remarried. She said she "refused to wash another man's dirty socks and underwear." Meanwhile, my grandfather decided that life on the other side wasn't so fun and asked my grandmother if he could come back home. Do you want to see how God can heal? She graciously allowed him to move back into the spare bedroom in her home, and she cared for him until he died of cancer the following year.

After my grandfather died, my grandmother didn't take many trips, but I took many to see her. We had amazing conversations and she taught me things that I still teach from the platform. She died several years ago, but *by allowing God to turn her brokenness to beauty,* she continues to affect thousands of women each time I share what I learned from her.

If you are experiencing brokenness today, I encourage you to **travel on**. Life may not have turned out the way you planned it, but taking a new trip with God may be just the vacation you need. Give Him the broken pieces and allow Him to reconstruct an image that reflects the light of His healing. Then, *enjoy the ride!*

Reflection

1. How do you cope when you go on an unexpected "ride" in your life?

2. Do you allow God to use the "brokenness" to expose beauty in your life or do you tend to harbor resentment and bitterness? How will you break the cycle if you harbor resentment and bitterness and allow God to use it for beauty in your life?

3. How do you handle injustice? Is God allowed to be your vindicator? If not, how will you allow Him to have this role in your life?

CHAPTER TEN

Four-Word Prayer

"This is the confidence we have in approaching God: that if we ask anything according to his will, he hears us. And if we know that he hears us—whatever we ask—we know that we have what we asked of him."
1 John 5:14-15 (NIV)

My husband, David, and I were in Colorado Springs visiting our son when we received a call that my father had suffered a heart attack. We packed our bags and flew home a day early to be with him, knowing that a hurricane by the name of "Ike" was also threatening to make landfall in Texas two days later.

As we walked into our home from the airport, the phone rang. "Ok, let's get it," my husband said boldly. As he hung up the phone, David turned to me and said, "Shannon that was the doctor. I have cancer."

My father, a hurricane, and now my husband—*a feeling of numbness overtook me.* It was as if my eyes wanted to explode with tears, but my stubbornness interceded. *Not now,* I thought. This was no time for breaking down.

I quietly ascended the stairs and snuggled into my

overstuffed "prayer chair." As I prepared to pour out my heart in formal declarations so that God would "really" hear me, the strangest thing happened. In place of eloquence came only four words: *"God, I trust you."*

Praying through hot tears for over an hour, the only words I could seem to whisper during my entire prayer time were the same, over and over again: *"God, I trust you."*

Can't I come up with anything better than this? I thought. After all, these were larger than life situations that needed larger than life prayers. That's when I heard four more words in my heart: *"Keep on pressing on."* It was as if the coach of my team had just stepped up to home plate while I was at bat and whispered in my ear, "You can do it! I'm right here with you."

A sudden **peace** came over me I could not explain, and I knew the cries of my heart had been heard. My prayer had been far from eloquent, but my four-word prayer had touched the very heart of God. He reminded me He would never leave, and that I could press on through each dilemma if I would take every step in faith with Him.

In the following week, Hurricane Ike made landfall. We were left with only a few fallen branches. During that same week, David's surgeons located the origin of his cancer and recommended a treatment that would ultimately leave him cancer-free while my father received two stints that left him healthier than he had been in years.

In the weeks that followed, one question resurfaced from friends, "How did you handle all of that at one time?" My response, *"I didn't."*

I had not handled any of it. I prayed a four-word prayer, and God did the rest. It sounds so simple, but it is so true. I found the answer in Isaiah 55:6 (NIV): *"Seek the Lord while He may be found. Call upon Him while He is near."*

God's Word never said I had to know the perfect way to pray. It only says to, "Seek Him and call on Him." That is what I did, and that is how I found the strength to press through each dilemma we faced. There was nothing special about my prayer, but it did come from the heart.

The result? God was faithful to His Word, and I saw Him do things as a result of my "hands off" approach. Not only did God allow me to see the amazing way He took over when I released the circumstances to Him, He also gave me a song to express what I experienced when I didn't know what to do. Each line serves as my continual reminder:

When the going gets tough,
keep on pressing on.
When the road is rough,
keep on moving on.

With each step along the way,

He will be your strength.
You're not alone;
He'll lead you home.

Keep on Pressing On.

Life seldom turns out the way we plan it, but there are MANY moments in our lives when God gets to show up and show out. When you only have a four-word prayer, know that it is enough to move the very throne of God to action. *Seek Him and call on His name.* He will do the rest to help you press into the very place He has just for you.

Reflection

1. Can you recall a time that God helped you "press on" when you had no idea what to do? Thank Him.

2. Is there a situation in your life where you need answers and there seem to be none? Ask Him.

3. Have you been in the middle of a difficult situation or are you in one now and you can see God's hand guiding you? Worship Him.

CHAPTER ELEVEN

All the Single Ladies

*"Oh Lord, you have searched me and you know me.
You know when I sit and when I rise; You perceive
my thoughts from afar." Psalm 139:1-2 (NIV)*

"You've got to date a lot of Volkswagens before you
find your Porsche."
- Author unknown

This chapter is dedicated to all of the single ladies. I would like to think I had the market cornered on this thought long before the pop singer Beyoncé got hold of it. Why? Because I have lived the life of a single lady and I am *well* acquainted with the blessings and challenges that it brings.

First of all, let me remind you that if you are single, you are just as important, valuable and meaningful as all the married ladies. I realize that some of you reading this may be perfectly content with remaining single, and that is fine. There are also some of you who would like to be married. That is fine too. I have found there are advantages to both.

When I was single, I thought about being married—A LOT. I just knew that once I got married, most of my problems would disappear. I had visions of waking up each morning as this wonderful man held me in his arms and adoringly told me how much he loved me. Then we would get up, have breakfast by candlelight, do our morning devotional together and pray. Afterward, we would be off to do our work for the day, but not before we stared into each other's eyes and told one another how we longed to be together again at the end of the day. During the day, there would be a surprise delivery of roses from him and I would rush home to make my husband his favorite dinner as a thank you for being the most wonderful man in the universe. After dinner, he would help me do the dishes because he couldn't wait to whisk me off to the bedroom and, well, you know…

After I woke up from the Barbie movie playing in my head, I realized that married life was just a **little** different than what I had envisioned. Don't get me wrong, there are some great advantages to being married and I wouldn't trade them for the world. There are also some great challenges. I can no longer have only Dr Pepper® and catsup in my refrigerator. Now that I am married, my refrigerator is in constant need of cleaning because of all of the cooking I do at home. Now my friends who knew me in my single days would never believe this, but take heart my friends, I *am* cooking. I no longer have the privilege of grabbing a burger at the drive-through without a thought of what someone else might want. I am married to a man who expects a fully cooked meal every night and if I do not deliver, it does not make for a happy evening in the Perry home. After all, this is the way he was raised.

Which brings me to another point. *Not only must we deal with our own baggage from days gone by, we will also deal with his.* We all have it, and we bring it into our marriages. I think this is why God said that marriage is for a lifetime. It takes that long to unpack all the "junk in our trunks." Marriage is a two-person show, FOREVER! Oh, we may think we can just get out if it doesn't work, but God's Word says that it is not that simple. According to the Bible, unless there is adultery or abandonment, we are in it for the long haul baby!

Did I also mention that you get to pay double the bills, wash double the clothes, clean double the mess and have double the heartache? After all, when you love someone as deeply as a husband, you can be hurt deeply as well.

Now I can hear some of my married friends saying, "Wow, that's a nice negative spin on marriage!" No, it is a *realistic* spin on marriage. There are many great things about marriage that the church teaches us, but somewhere along the way, many of our single ladies are receiving the message that once they get married, their lives will miraculously turn around. I know because I meet many at my conferences that tell me this is what they believe.

I am sure that single ladies get as tired of hearing what I am about to say as I do of saying it, but here goes:

Marriage is not intended to make us a whole person. That is what Jesus does. We are not a bunch of "half people" walking around looking for someone to make us whole when we are single. We are whole because of the life we live for Christ. Therefore, marriage is designed to make us holy more than it is to make us "whole" and happy.

Many women tell me that they are looking for a man to "complete" them. May I tell you that I believed this lie for a long time? I believed that until I found the "right one," there was a missing part of me somewhere. This is a lie that the enemy would love for you to believe. *You are complete because of what Jesus did on the cross.* PERIOD! There is no other man who will ever "complete" you except Jesus.

So what about that constant urge that won't go away? You want to be married and you want to have children. You do not feel God has called you to a single life, yet no one is showing up, and it isn't for a lack of looking! One phrase I heard quite often in my single days was, "Just pray about it. God will bring you the right one." I always wanted to laugh when someone said this and respond, "That seems like all I do these days!" The truth is, *prayer really is the most important thing you can do for finding God's will in this area of your life.* Then we have to take our hands off and accept what He does as a result. This can be the difficult part, but it is vitally important.

I know if you are single and really want to be married,

you are most likely spending countless hours on your face before God. Do yourself a favor and leave it there. *Stop trying so hard.* You are wearing yourself out and if God says it is not time for you to have a mate, you can kick and scream all day but it will not bring your man any sooner. When God is ready to give him to you, there will be nothing that can stop him. Let me repeat that. Nothing can stop God's man from coming into your life when you are praying and trusting God for him. *So relax.* Give yourself and God a break. God's clock is not broken and He is not worried about your biological clock. Remember Sarah? We are talking about God here. The One who made you, who formed you and the One who knows what you need.

Think of being in training. Every day is a fresh start to train for God's purpose. This could be the most exciting ride of your life, so stay in the game. *Stop obsessing over "the man" and get your eyes on "The Man."* He is the One who completes you, and when you are complete in Him, look out! Your life will be more exciting than you ever dreamed as He brings His plan to completion.

When you are discouraged read Psalm 139:1-18. He knows where you are, He knows what you need, He planned each day out before you were born and there is nowhere you can go that He will forget you. He loves His single ladies!

Reflection

1. If you are single, how do you handle waiting on God's answer for your life?

2. What are the biggest challenges you face as a single lady? Go to God and ask Him to fill the void that you feel.

3. What are some activities that you can participate in that will help you meet Godly, Christian friends who will support and encourage you?

CHAPTER TWELVE

The Rest of the Story

"Trust in the Lord with all your heart and lean not on your own understanding. In all your ways acknowledge Him, and He will make your paths straight." Proverbs 3:5-6 (NIV)

As I travel, I love to tell the story of how I met my husband and son. Oh, yes, I tell the wonderful events of teaching Sean in first grade, and how his dad and I reconnected after fourteen years and became engaged. The part I *rarely* tell is what happened in my life in the months prior to reconnecting with David.

I was introduced to a man in the single's group at my church when I was in my mid-thirties and was told he was interested in taking me out. Being a single Christian woman who *desperately wanted to be married,* I prayed a five-minute prayer and decided that this must be God's way of bringing a man into my life. After all, he was good looking *and* he was an attorney. This had to be God!

We went out for dinner and began dating. As the weeks turned into months, I began to really care for this man and he seemed to care deeply for me as well. Not long into our relationship, I was whisked away to another world when he took me to dinner one night and asked me to be his wife. I quickly responded with a "Yes" and thanked God that He had moved in such a timely way on my behalf. I was finally getting married! I was so happy. I began imagining living in his house, becoming a stepmom to his three beautiful children and began planning for my new life as his wife.

Then, disaster struck…

Two months into our engagement, my fiancé said that he wasn't sure that he wanted to get married. At first I thought he was kidding, but seeing the bewildered look on his face, I realized this was no joke. I began to panic, asking him what I had done and how I could do things differently to change his mind? All he could tell me is that *I had done nothing wrong.* How could that be? He went from asking me to spend my life with him to telling me he wasn't sure he wanted to be married. There must be **something** I had done so there must be **something** I could do to fix it.

He told me there was nothing I could do and asked me to give him a couple of weeks. Broken-hearted and bewildered, I agreed to do so. I spent my Spring Break in Florida with some girlfriends from work and what should have been a wonderful adventure was one of the worst weeks of my life. I am sure my friends were ready to throw me to the sharks as I paced during our entire vacation waiting to hear my fiancé's decision. *I could have never been prepared for the answer.*

Upon returning from Florida, I met my fiancé for dinner. The rides at Six Flags could not have made me feel more nauseous as I entered the restaurant. We exchanged pleasantries and he quickly got to the point. After two weeks of pondering his decision, he said he felt he could not marry me. *I tried to remain calm.* I had visions of snatching the tablecloth and dishes from the table like you see in the movies as my emotions began to unravel. I wanted to know why! He never told me. He just continued to say that he didn't feel like "it was right."

Devastated and heartbroken, I took the ring from my finger and handed it to him. I stood up, thanked him for being honest, and made my way to the door. To add insult to injury, I ran into the glass door as I was leaving the restaurant. I could not seem to focus on anything... including what was in front of me.

Driving home from the restaurant, I shook violently as I cried out to God, *"WHY?! Why now? Why this? After all this time that I have prayed for someone to love me, why?"* That seemed to be the only question I could ask, and I grieved until I thought my heart would pop out of my chest.

In the days to follow, I lay on my couch and did nothing. My diet consisted of Ritz® crackers and Dr Pepper®. The only time I got up was to let my dog out. Two ladies from the singles group stopped by to check on me after hearing I was going through a tough time. I kindly thanked them for their visit, but told them nothing of what had happened. After all, how could I explain it to anyone when I really didn't understand it myself?

On the third day of my "couch sabbatical," my telephone rang. The voice on the other end sounded bewildered and depressed. It was another man from our singles group who said that he needed to talk to me. I could tell by the tone in his voice that I was about to hear much more than a "testimony." *My heart was NOT prepared for what came next.*

He told me that he and my fiancé had gone to the movies while I was in Florida. While there, my fiancé made a "pass" at him. *"They must have played football,"* I thought to myself. No other kind of "pass" even entered my mind. He went on to tell me that as the night together progressed, the two of them had become sexually involved.

I don't quite recall if I fell off the couch and hit my head or stood up and then fell over, but somehow I remember landing on the floor. This same man that was prepared to vow his life to me had been sexually involved with another man? I tried to keep my composure as the other man began to cry and offer his apologies. I told him that God was the one who needed the apology, not me. I was angry, hurt, betrayed and confused, but at some point in our conversation, *God gave me tremendous compassion for this man.* I encouraged him to call our pastor and get counseling. At the end of the call, I prayed that God would heal him from this horrible experience and quietly hung up the phone.

Staring into space, I sat in disbelief as I tried to process the conversation. Then, I heard God's voice. It wasn't an audible voice. It was that still, small voice inside my heart. As I listened closely He said, *"Shannon, you asked me why I did this TO you? I want you to know, I was never IN this."* I had wanted something so badly, that I jumped ahead of God and caused myself a lot of heartache in the process. God was faithful, however, and protected me from disaster. Just as we warn our children when they reach for a hot stove, God was screaming, *"The burner is ON baby. Get away from the stove!"*

Though the days to follow were filled with various emotions, one thing was unchanging: God's willingness to go to any lengths to protect me. *He will do the same for you!* Proverbs 3:5-6 reminds us that we can trust Him no matter what the circumstances may be. We may not understand why He does things until we reach Heaven, but one thing is for sure: *we can trust Him.* As He carries us through those days of Ritz® crackers and Dr Pepper®, we can take heart that He will not put us down until He brings us to a place of safety.

Maybe you find yourself in an unbelievable place today. A friend has betrayed you, a spouse has walked out on you, or a disease has gripped a loved one and left you wondering why. Remember what

Proverbs 3:5-6 says, *"...lean not on your own under-standing; in all your ways acknowledge Him... "* (NIV) Allow God to know that you are hurting, angry, disappointed, upset. He can handle it. The Bible never says, "Do not grieve." It only says, *"...do not grieve like the rest of men, who have no hope." (1 Thessalonians 4:13 NIV)* As long as Jesus lives, there is hope in your circumstance. It may not turn out the way that you had originally planned, but take heart, *"All things work together for good to those who love God." (Romans 8:28 NIV)*

Let go of trying to handle the situation on your own and trying to figure things out. Instead, ask God to help you come to a place of peace so that you are able to say, "God, whatever is going on here, I am letting go of trying to figure this out and I am going to trust you." There is such freedom in letting go. After we do that, we can claim the final part of Proverbs 3:6 which says, *"...and He will make your paths straight."* God may not do things the way we would, but when we put our trust in Him, He will make our paths straight. He did for me.

After grieving for a period of time, I left the Ritz® crackers and Dr. Pepper® behind and went to see my Grandmother. We talked about what had happened, and in the process, she asked me if there was anyone I would be interested in. I told her I believed my "picker" might be broken, and that unless God revealed Mr. Wonderful out of the blue, I would remain single. "There's not one that comes to mind?" she asked. Suddenly, I remembered calling David for a swimming pool bid while my fiancé and I were engaged. During the course of our conversation, David asked me if I was still single. I told my Grandmother the story, and her response was, "Oh, we like the pool man."

After my Grandmother's encouragement and prodding, I managed to gain the confidence to call David a second time. I didn't have the heart to tell him why I was "single again," but he was so happy to hear it, he didn't care. God didn't care either. God used the situation that was meant for evil, and turned it around for my good. God kept David and Sean waiting in the wings until the time was right to give them to me. He not only protected me from disaster, He gave me a new family.

And as the late radio host, Paul Harvey, used to say, *"**That** is the rest of the story."*

Reflection

1. Name a time in your life when God protected you from hidden danger or disappointment. Thank Him for His faithfulness in your circumstance.

2. How can you "let go" of things that are hurting you today?

3. Is there anything in your life that is keeping you from trusting God with every circumstance you are facing? Ask Him to remove any obstacles that stand in the way of putting all your faith in Him.

CHAPTER THIRTEEN

Those Glittering Tears

"You have kept count of my tossings; put my tears in your bottle. Are they not in your book?" Psalm 56:8 (ESV)

As I stood in aisle three of the local Hobby Lobby, I could hardly contain myself. While shoppers briskly passed me humming tunes of Christmas joy, I stood among the Christmas trim crying my eyes out. *"Shannon, get it together,"* I thought. "How could anyone be so sad in the middle of all this joy?" Christmas is "the most wonderful time of the year" after all. This year, I had volunteered to get the Christmas flowers and decorate my grandparents' graves. My maternal and paternal grandparents are buried in a large cemetery within yards of one another. We drive four hours from home each year to place Christmas flowers and a special ornament on their tombstones. Christmas was always a very special time with them and I still recall amazing memories.

As *"I'll be Home for Christmas"* streamed through the store's speakers, I wiped the tears from my face. With each stem of flowers I chose, I remembered the wonderful times I shared with my Grandparents. I also remembered how much I missed them. I tried desperately to fight the tears then finally gave up. So what if someone sees me crying? I am sure they could relate to missing someone at this time of year. The clerk who helped me with my purchases blew my cover when she asked, "Are you alright?" I thought, *"That was odd. Was she a mind reader? How did she know?"* So I smiled a sheepish smile and answered, "Yes."

When I got in my car, I quickly discovered the answer. I had left a trail of glitter on my face from wiping my tears after holding flowers full of glitter-filled leaves. It looked like a snow globe had exploded on my head. I laughed out loud and found it comforting that *even when I feel sad there was still a joy that could not be taken from me.*

Many things can bring about difficult emotions during holidays, anniversaries or the birthday of one we have loved and lost. Some of these triggers include unresolved guilt, past losses, anticipating a significant loss or disappointment with a current situation. A very common trigger during yearly celebrations is the grief of past loss or the anticipation of another. This is a very real experience and we must treat it as such. We have a Comforter who understands our weaknesses and He promises to help us each moment. From my many years of counseling, I learned that when people are willing to face grief and deal with it constructively, the agonizing pain could subside. When dealing with grief from a loss, it is helpful to remember the following:

- *It is ok to cry.* As one of my favorite songs says, "Tears are a language that God understands." He understood mine in aisle three of Hobby Lobby.

- *Do not try to over exert yourself* when you are grieving. Set reasonable expectations for what you will do and allow yourself to receive as well as give.

- *Create one new tradition for your yearly celebration* as you treasure and respect existing ones. This often makes the transition easier and there is less guilt over moving on from or changing standing traditions too quickly.

- *Remember that it is only one day out of the year.* It does not determine the rest of your life. Jesus does.

- *Do one thing that you really enjoy.* Get a new haircut, take a bubble bath, or read a book you have been longing to read.

- *Talk to one person that you feel safe with* and let them know how much you value your relationship with them. If you cannot think of one person, allow that to be a new goal for you. Ask God to bring you the friend He has chosen just for you.

If you or someone you know is struggling beyond the blues into the grip of depression, it is important to seek help immediately. Depression left untreated is not only unhealthy it is dangerous. Recently, a dear friend of mine lost her daughter in a way most parents can never fathom. She knew her daughter was upset, but did not understand many of the underlying issues. In one dark moment, her daughter listened to the lies in her own mind and she ended her life abruptly. If someone you know mentions "wanting to die," take it *very* seriously. One can never be too careful and it is best to err on the side of caution. Should you hear someone say this, inform his or her family or law enforcement. Make someone aware that you are concerned.

If you have feelings of not wanting to live, seek out immediate attention from others. They do care and they want to help. You are not alone in this battle. Not only are there others who care, your Creator has *"plans to prosper you and not to harm you..."* *(Jeremiah 29:11 NIV)* He reminds us that we are *"fearfully and wonderfully made,"* *(Psalm 139:14 NIV)* and that we *"can do ALL things through Christ who strengthens"* us. *(Philippians 4:13 NKJV)*

Do not allow the lies of your emotions to rule. Ask God to help you in the areas that are difficult. Pray that your expectations are only those that He would have you hold, then keep the focus on the One who gave His life just for you. He has *never* forgotten you.

Allow the giver of all good gifts to redefine your celebrations this year. He gave the most celebrated gift in history. Accept it and know that His presence in your life is very real. He sees every tear that falls, even ones that glitter.

Reflection

1. How do you handle the emotions that accompany the anniversary of one you have loved and lost?

2. Have you given yourself permission to grieve a loss you have experienced?

3. What is a new tradition that you can use to honor one you have loved and lost?

SHANNON PERRY

CHAPTER FOURTEEN

Broken Pieces

"The sacrifices of God are a broken spirit; a broken and contrite heart, O God, you will not despise." Psalm 51:17 (NIV)

Ⓞne of my greatest weaknesses is my eating habits. I love everything that is unhealthy, so when my assistant recently suggested that we have soup and salad for lunch, I hid in front of my computer and made an ugly face. *Yuck*, I thought. *Who wants to have salad when you can have a burger and fries?* While I dearly love my assistant, I am not nearly as fond of salad. As a matter of fact, salad on a plate reminds me of what I see when I empty my lawnmower bag: a lot of grass with some "weedy looking" things thrown in. I reluctantly agreed to go to the local bistro for lunch after remembering they also serve pizza.

After placing our order at the counter, we headed to the back of the restaurant to find a table. An attractive blonde caught my attention from the corner of the restaurant. She was wearing really cute clothes, so I glanced to get a closer look at what she had on. Her face was strangely familiar. *All of a sudden, my heart rose in my chest.* This familiar face had made a **very** significant impact in my life and though she had no idea who I was, I certainly recognized her. It was well-known author and speaker, Beth Moore. Like an excited little girl at Disney World, I leaned across the table, grabbed my assistant by the arm and whispered, *"Laurie, is that Beth Moore?"* Laurie took one look and said, "Yep, sure is." I could hardly contain myself. Beth's books had taken me through some of the darkest days of my life, and now I was having lunch in the same restaurant with her! I was so glad *I* had chosen this restaurant and that salad was on the menu for the day.

After we finished eating Laurie and I prepared to leave. As we headed toward the door, we passed Beth's table. She was leaning over having a very intimate conversation with the young lady she was with, so I hated to interrupt her, but I did it anyway! I could not miss the chance to tell her what an impact she had made in my life. If it were not for some of the things I learned through her writing, I might not be singing, speaking or even writing this book.

I slipped into the booth beside Beth, apologized for my interruption and began to tell her what an influence she had been in my life. She was extremely gracious as she hugged me and introduced me to her lunch date. It was her daughter Amanda. I introduced Laurie, and we all had a beautiful time talking. Beth hugged me several times, and even said how proud she was of me for the work I was doing. *Wow*, I thought to myself. *Beth Moore is proud of me?* I had never been so happy to be at a restaurant that served salad!

As we got ready to leave, Beth noticed the purse I was carrying and complimented it. *I wanted to crawl under the table.* Here I was face to face with Beth Moore and little did she know I had broken the strap to my purse just before we came into the restaurant. I tried to tuck the broken strap inside the purse and hide it but the bulge protruding from the side gave it away. Neither Beth nor Amanda seemed to notice as they continued with their compliments. Then it happened. Beth began touching the purse. *No!* I thought. Beth Moore was touching **my** purse and I needed to have it all together. If she continued touching it, she would feel the broken strap. *I couldn't hide it anymore.* I broke down and told them about the broken piece and how I was carrying the purse by one good strap so no one would know it was broken. *I will never forget Beth's response.* "Well Shannon, I think it is adorable just the way it is and I would carry it just like that." Imagine, Beth Moore loved me and my broken purse! This woman was just like Jesus.

I modeled the various ways one could carry the broken purse and we all got a good laugh. I thanked Beth and Amanda for their time, we hugged once more, and left the restaurant. I thanked Laurie all the way back to the office for her wonderful choice of lunch that day.

I thought about my encounter later that evening and

realized how blessed I had been to feel so loved by someone despite my broken pieces. Beth had been a living example of Jesus as she embraced me when I shared some of the struggles I had experienced and then found ways to make the "broken pieces" become a positive in my life. *Isn't this just like Jesus?* He embraces us when we come to Him as we are and He finds ways to do great things with our broken pieces.

The Bible gives several examples of beauty coming from broken things. Take Jacob, for example? It was not until Jacob's natural strength was broken and his *"hip was wrenched"* at Peniel in Genesis 32:25 that he came to the point where God anointed him with spiritual strength. In Luke 9:16, the miracle of feeding five thousand with two loaves of bread and five fish did not occur until Jesus took "the five loaves...*and broke them.*" It was through the very process of the loaves being broken that the miracle occurred. Once Mary *broke* her beautiful "alabaster jar of very expensive perfume" in Matthew 26:7, the true value was revealed.

God uses broken things. Today, humbly allow Him to take every broken piece of your life. Don't try to fake it or hide it. Release your brokenness to Him and watch what happens. If God can use a broken strap on my purse to bring such a precious encounter as He did with Beth, think of all the wonderful things He can do when you *allow Him to invade your broken spaces.*

Although I didn't want to eat at the bistro, God allowed me to have a beautiful experience once I was there. If God is calling you to go to a place you don't really want to go in your spiritual life, GO! You never know what surprise He has in store.

Reflection

1. What are some broken pieces of your life that you have attempted to hide?

2. Recall a time that you released all your brokenness to God. How did He turn the broken pieces into something beautiful?

3. Today, turn all your broken pieces over to God in prayer. Allow Him to invade every broken area.

SHANNON PERRY

Section III

Lacing Up the

Tongue

"A lie can travel halfway around the world
while the truth is still putting on its shoes."
- Mark Twain -

"Words"

From the CD "The Real Thing"
© 2009 Paul Marino and Shannon Perry

They can steal your heart or set you free
They can make you doubt or make you believe
They can churn the waves or calm the sea
They can be a best friend or worst enemy

Words they have a way
Of showing love or spewing hate
They can build you up or tear you down
Take you in or throw you out
Words they have a way
Of dowsing fires or fanning flames
So be careful what you say
Cause words have a way

They can let you know that you fit in
Or make you feel like giving in
They can be a summer breeze or a winter wind
They can steal your trust or bring it back again

Words they have a way
Of showing love or spewing hate
They can build you up or tear you down
Take you in or throw you out
Words they have a way
Of dowsing fires or fanning flames
So be careful what you say
Cause words have a way

And once they're out,
You can't get 'em back
No you can't get 'em back
No, no

Words they have a way
Of showing love or spewing hate
They can build you up or tear you down
Take you in or throw you out
Words they have a way
Of dowsing fires or fanning flames

So be careful what you say
Oh be careful what you say
Be careful what you say
Cause words have a way

CHAPTER FIFTEEN

To Judge or Not to Judge

"Dear friends, do not believe every spirit, but test the spirits to see whether they are from God, because many false prophets have gone out into the world." 1 John 4:1 (NIV)

It takes **a lot** to make me nervous. I rarely get nervous when I have television interviews or speaking engagements, but there is something that can really make my pulse race—*singing at weddings and funerals.* That may sound funny, but both of these are very emotional days for people and I cringe at the thought of doing anything that might make their event more stressful. Like forgetting the words to a song—or worse, singing the wrong song.

When I shared my apprehensions about weddings and funerals with a friend of mine, *he laughed.* He is a worship leader at a large church here in my hometown and has sung at so many weddings and funerals, I get hives just thinking about it! I felt a little silly about my fears until he called me one day to tell me his latest story.

"Mr. Funeral Singer" was asked to sing at the funeral of one of the senior citizens from his church that passed away. When he asked the widow what she would like sung, her response was shocking. "Jingle

Bells. My husband's favorite song, was Jingle Bells."
"Jingle Bells?" my friend asked in disbelief. He heard
correctly. The little lady repeated herself with a slight
hint of frustration. "Jingle Bells."

In the middle of July with over four hundred people
in attendance, my friend stood at the funeral and sang
every verse and chorus of "Jingle Bells." Anyone
who happened to be distracted was immediately
tuned in to this service. What would they do next?
Throw snowballs?

After the funeral, the little widow approached my
friend. She tapped him on the arm and whispered in
his ear, "Honey, you did a very nice job, but did I tell
you to sing 'Jingle Bells'?" Hesitant to respond, my
friend said, *"Why, yes you did."* She said, "Oh dear.
I meant 'When They Ring Those Golden Bells'!"

My friend apologized for judging my fears and agreed
that *anything* could happen while singing at such a
special engagement.

The word **judgment** is used throughout the Bible. It
has a great deal to say about being judgmental, but
what does that really mean? Are we never to judge
anything? What if we see something and we know it
is wrong? Are we to overlook it and not have an
opinion about it?

After researching, I have found that there is a verse in
the Bible we need to consider when we look at the
word judgment. Come with me to 1 Thessalonians
5:21-22. It reads: *"Test everything. Hold on to the*

good. Avoid every kind of evil." (NIV) The Bible addresses two types judgment that are worth studying.

The first type of judging is "Good Judging." This is where we identify the spirit that is behind the action.

"Dear Friends, do not believe every spirit, but test the Spirits to see if they are from God." 1 John 4:1 (NIV)

If the actions of a person bring glory to God, then the spirit behind that person is of God. Seems pretty simple, right?

Where things seem to get more complicated is in the realm of "pop spiritualism." The word "spirituality" is being taken and used in many things, and they are not all Christian things.

Allow me to get on my beautifully decorated soapbox for a moment. As I minister at events, I shudder when I hear someone say the word "spirituality." Unfortunately, we have become so addicted to being comfortable that many in our society have decided that the Bible may not be Absolute Truth. In fact, some say we are so powerful as "spiritual beings" that we have the right to take God's Word and add or take away from it as long as it makes us feel good. My sweet friend, *this is a lie* from the very pit of Hell itself. In case you have not looked it up, allow me to enlighten you. The word "spirituality" is also found with the definition of the religion Wicca. Wicca is the religion that worships Satan. Feeling more cautious about the use of "spirituality" now?

I say all of that to say this. When we are talking about the word judgment as Christians, there are some things that we have an obligation to judge. All judgment is not bad.

"Have nothing to do with the fruitless deeds of darkness, but rather expose them." Ephesians 5:11 (NIV)

If we are to discern between good and evil, some judgment will be involved.

While we are never to set ourselves up to play God, we are called to follow His lead and *"...be as wise as serpents and innocent as doves." (Matthew 10:16 ESV)* There are many who may call themselves Christians, but if they are continually living contrary to the Word of God or telling you things that are not in the Word of God, BEWARE!

There is also a form of "Bad Judging" that we must consider and Jesus warns us against. In Matthew 7:1-5, Jesus addresses *those who are using the same sin that they are guilty of to belittle another person.* He clearly states that this is wrong. Paul echoes this point   in Romans 2:1-4. When we use a person's sin as a bat over their head, it is wrong. So is confronting someone about their sin without following up with encouragement. Many times in the church we see those who are so damaged by the damnation they receive from church leaders that they never want to have anything to do with Christianity again. This, my friend, is wrong and it breaks God's heart.

"For God did not send His Son into the world to condemn the world, but that the world through Him might be saved." John 3:17 (NKJV)

If you are the victim of bad judging please hear me today. Jesus is not standing by waiting for you to mess up so He can judge you then knock you over the head. His nature is love and it is to be our nature as Christians. If you have been hurt by someone who calls themself a Christian, be reminded that *Christians are fallible people in need of a Savior.* We mess up every day and we often get it wrong but Jesus NEVER gets it wrong!

RUN to Him with everything you have knowing that as you run toward Him, He is already running to you. Ask Him to help you forgive those who may have hurt you with judgmental comments. Then ask Him to help you walk wisely, loving only those things that He loves.

Reflection

1. Have you ever been a victim of someone's judgmental comments? How did you handle the situation?

2. Have you been guilty of judging someone in the wrong way? What can you do to follow up and make it right?

3. How will you handle a situation when God calls you to judge a situation that is in violation to His Word?

4. To learn more of what God's Word says about judgment, read the following passages:

   I Thessalonians 5:21-22
   2 Timothy 3:16-17
   Titus 2:15
   Ephesians 5:11
   1 Corinthians 2:15-16
   Matthew 7:1-5
   Luke 6:41-42

CHAPTER SIXTEEN

Slimy Slander

"You shall not bear a false report; do not join your hand with a wicked man to be a malicious witness." Exodus 23:1 (NASB)

Slander. Just the sound of the word reminds me of something slimy, like the snake that slithered across my foot the other day in the pasture. I was walking along, minding my own business, when out of nowhere he shot across my foot like a rocket. I never saw him coming and hardly saw him going. I screeched for David who was in the barn with the tractor motor roaring. He never knew I was in danger. I thought about going after Mr. Slimy with the hoe, and then I thought better of it. Why hunt something you really don't want to find? I **do not** like snakes.

Maybe you have had Mr. (or Ms.) Slimy enter your territory unannounced. You were walking along minding your own business, when out of nowhere they slithered into your world with slander. You know if you have been slandered. It is that destructive, cutting remark that seers your soul and dives into the very heart of who you are. They search for a kink in your armor, and if they can't find one, they create one. Then, they prepare for the kill.

"Whoever conceals hatred with lying lips and spreads slander is a fool." Proverbs 10:18 (NIV)

A fool is someone who is right in his or her own eyes, and takes no account that they could ever be wrong. When a fool begins to slander, he believes there is one absolute truth... his.

So why do people slander? Simple. They usually want what you have. They are envious of your accomplishments, looks, job, talent, connections, and the list goes on. Simply stated, they feel something is missing in their life and they see it in yours. Then they find something wrong with you so that they can somehow feel better about themselves.

The Bible gives great insight into the lives of wise men and fools in Matthew 7:24-27. While the wise man builds his house upon the rock, the fool builds his on the sand. Rock is solid. Sand is not. Wise men are solid. Fools are not. I learned a song about this when I was young, but it has taken on an entirely new meaning since becoming an adult. One truth that wise men and women understand is this: *Diminishing the image of another will never enhance our own image.*

When we feel insecure about an area of our life, we have choices to make. We can do as the fool does and begin throwing stones at everyone else's house or we can sit down and evaluate our insecurity. The exercise class at my gym (which I should attend much more frequently) seems to find the most attractive and fit ladies I have ever seen. One of them is even named Barbie! When I see them, I have a choice to make. Do I give them the once over, just hoping to find a roll on them somewhere? Or do I think, "Wow, they have really worked at this and they look great. Maybe I should work a little harder myself!" May I be honest with you? There have been days that I was so hoping to see a roll on their stomach when they were doing sit-ups. Surely if you are crunching all that flesh together you can conger up some fat somewhere! Nothing. Their stomachs were as flat then as when they were standing up. That's when I decided to do the work or stop trying to find the kink.

But what if I have worked as hard as the other person and they still get the advantage? Good news. Isaiah 14:27 says, *"The Lord of Heaven's Armies has spoken—who can change his plans? When his hand is raised, who can stop him?"* (NLT) There is no reason for us to snuff out another person's light so that ours will burn brighter. When we really trust that God's plans are in place in our lives, we know that no man can thwart the purpose God has for us. Therefore, we have no reason to worry about what is going on in someone else's life because we are so tuned in to what He is doing in our own.

If the slanderous tongue has seared your soul, I have good news for you. *God is well able to vindicate you.* A pastor friend taught me a very valuable lesson about dealing with slander. After being shepherd over his congregation for years, this pastor was being viciously and inappropriately accused of things that were simply not true. Some people in his church were upset over a decision, and they were determined to cause dissension by finding some kinks in the pastor's armor. When there were none to be found, they created some.

The pastor and I were talking one day and I asked him how he could remain so quiet about all the slanderous gossip. The things that were being said were ludicrous, and I could not imagine the heartache he must be going through knowing the betrayal he was facing. I will never forget his response. He turned to me and with a smile on his face responded, "Shannon, you say nothing. Then when it's all over, you know the only one who has spoken is God." This was a wise man responding to a group of destructive fools.

Just as I was tempted to go after the snake, we are often tempted to go after those who slander us. But just like the snake, why hunt something that you really don't want to find? *Allow God to expose them.* That is what my pastor friend did, and he was right. Months after our talk, the fools gave up as their lies began to be exposed and they eventually left the church. His church continues to be one of the largest congregations in the United States.

God will make a way when there seems to be no way. We just have to stay out of the way.

Reflection

1. Has anyone ever slandered you? What was their motive?

2. Have you ever slandered someone? What was your motive?

3. Ask God to forgive you if you have slandered someone. If someone has slandered you, ask God to heal you and help you to stay out of the way as He handles the situation.

CHAPTER SEVENTEEN

The Nasty Chain

"What goes into someone's mouth does not defile them, but what comes out of their mouth, that is what defiles them." Matthew 15:11 (NIV)

Words. They have torn down empires and formed agreements that built nations. They have made commitments at the altar and sealed the fate of marriages on divorce papers. They have formed the best of friendships and made the worst of enemies. Words are powerful, and once they're out, we can never get them back. We can say we're sorry. We can ask God's forgiveness and we can truly be repentant, but once they have been spoken, they have been deposited somewhere.

Sometimes our words are empty and don't count for much. They are left floating around in the air and no one thinks much of them. Sometimes our words are funny. This is where I prefer to live. I love to see people laugh. There is something about saying something to bring a smile to someone else that I live for. Sometimes our words go deeper. They are deposited in the very soul of another and may live there for years, even a lifetime. Maybe this is why Jesus has so much to say about the condition of our heart. The tongue only produces a physical manifestation of what is really in our heart. We know this to be true because the Bible says, *"...For out of the abundance of the heart, the mouth speaketh."* (Matthew 12:34 KJV) Words, they have a way.

When I was five-years-old, I grew up being called "Big Mama" by the kids on my block. Oh, I can laugh more about it now, but just writing it brings back memories of the days I spent crying to Mom and Dad when the kids made fun of me. The problem was, I believed them! I took to heart everything they said, let it take root on the inside of me, and as a result I grew up believing that I was ugly and unlovable. Never mind that I was a finalist in beauty pageants and being asked to model. I allowed what had been said to me to become truth. Has that ever happened to you?

Sometimes the words that are spoken to us are those that we can brush aside, think nothing of and let roll off our back. Other times, they linger in our minds and we mull over them for days, months and even years. We do this for many reasons but I have found the main reason I do it is to try to understand. *Why* did that person say what he or she said? Now I have been told, as you get older you stop caring as much about this kind of thing, so I am happy to say I must still be young because I still think about it—sometimes, to my detriment. When someone has spoken a hurtful word to me, I tend to dwell. I think about what they said, what I should have said in return, and well, you know the drill. Recently, God has changed my way of thinking.

I have learned to take to heart what God says about the heart. Whatever condition a person's heart is in, you will know when they open their mouth. For example, we can be having a terrible day, but if our heart is in the right place, we understand that there is no place in scripture that justifies our being nasty to someone because our day has been bad. The problem is, nasty is the gift that keeps on giving. Once someone is nasty to us, we can take it to heart and then it becomes rooted on the inside of us. Next thing you know, we are nasty to someone else. They take our unkind words to heart, let them become rooted on the inside of them, and then they are nasty to the next person. Before you know it, the "nasty chain" has grown into thirty people and we were the first link on the chain. Since I don't want to be the entrepreneur of the "nasty chain," I have to be the end of the chain. In other words, when someone is nasty to me, it stops with me. This is when my flesh wants to scream, "No!" but my Spirit says, "Now you're talking."

If you have ever been wearing a necklace when one of the links breaks, you know it is impossible to keep the necklace on. If you try, it falls off because the piece needed to hold it together is no longer available. It is the same with us. If someone is nasty to you, break the chain by refusing to be the same way to others.

Sometimes, I make this a game for myself. When someone speaks hurtful words to me, I make it a point to be nice to the next person I see. Guess what? They are usually nice in return! The challenge comes when I am nice to the next person and they don't reciprocate. Inside my head, four words come to mind, "Here we go baby." Inside my heart, however, is that still small voice that says, "**Break** the chain."

So what do you say? Will you be a broken link or will you continue the chain? The choice is yours. God says, *"because you are lukewarm, and neither hot nor cold, I will spit you out of My mouth." (Revelation 3:16 NASB)* Kind of a gruesome picture of how He feels about the chain, but he minces no words. God's will is that when you are mistreated by words; do not allow them to take root in your Spirit. Instead, evaluate and do not dwell on them. If there is validity to what has been spoken, address it immediately. If there is no validity, do not allow it to take root. Send it on an imaginary balloon right back up to God and let Him deal with the heart of that person. And yes, even pray for them. Ask God to help heal the heart out of which they speak so that no more damage is done. Then, let it go and get on with the joy of being kind with your words.

When others hurt us with their words, God will intervene on our behalf when we keep our mouth closed. I know personally. Remember the kids that used to make fun of me? I ran into some of them not too long ago and all they could talk about was how beautiful I was and how proud they were of what I was doing with my life.

God always has the ultimate word, and what He says, stands.

Reflection

1. What will you do when hurtful words are spoken to you?

2. How important is it for you to rid yourself of bitterness and resentment when hurtful words are spoken? How can you let go?

3. Ask God to heal anything in your heart that may cause you to participate in the "nasty chain." Ask Him to bring healing where hurtful words have been spoken.

CHAPTER EIGHTEEN

The Pretty Tongue

"A gossip betrays a confidence, but a trustworthy person keeps a secret." Proverbs 11:13 (NIV)

Do you remember that old show "Hee-Haw?" It was a variety show that offered comedy, music and fun. Every Saturday evening, Mom, Dad and I would tune in. I loved singing the following words with the ladies on the show:

> *We're not ones to go around spreading rumors.*
> *No really we're just not the gossipy kind.*
> *No, you'll never hear one of us repeating gossip.*
> *So you'd better be sure and listen close the first time.*

Gossip wasn't gossip... as long as they didn't repeat it.

When I am teaching the topic of "Lacing Up the Tongue" at our **If the Shoe Fits** events, the topic of gossip often drives women to the ladies room. Why? Because as women, it just seems to come so, well, natural for us. After all it is not often you hear two men ask, "Did you see what Bill was wearing last week?" They don't care!

There are several reasons that we as women often get entangled in gossip. Once we understand the reasons we gossip and the consequences gossip brings, it is much easier to break this habit and use our words for more productive means.

One reason we participate in gossip is that *it makes us feel special.* When we have access to information others want that translates to power. We often resort to gossip as a means of having more control when we are feeling powerless in other parts of our lives. After all, there is a certain importance we feel when someone asks, "How did you know that?" One problem. We have just drawn water from a dry well. The approval and attention we receive from knowing "important information" soon disappear and we are left to deal with the consequences when someone finds out we have betrayed their confidence.

Gossip also gives us something to talk about *besides our own problems.* Let's face it. It is often easier to sit around and discuss what others should do with their problems than discuss solutions for our own. Unfortunately, this does not make our problems disappear, and we are left to deal with our own issues in the hollows of our minds.

So why does the Bible warn us to stay away from gossip? Proverbs 18:8 says, *"The words of a gossip are like choice morsels; they go down to a man's [and woman's] inmost parts." (NIV)* According to this verse, gossip doesn't just bounce off us. It goes down to the inmost parts of our heart and affects US much more than the one about whom we are gossiping. When our tongue is used to "bite" others, we are the ones who wind up with the teeth marks.

Have you ever been involved in a gossip ring? It doesn't take long for the fur to fly. For example, you go to lunch with several girlfriends. At first the conversation is innocent until one by one others begin to add "what they know." By the time lunch is over, you know much more than you wanted to know and said much more than you needed to say. I have been there, on the giving and receiving end.

Several years ago God greeted me one morning during my quiet time with some wise words about gossip. He made it very clear how I would know if I were gossiping or not. If the person or situation you are discussing is not represented in the room, squeeze your lips together and don't open them! It's pretty simple to understand and much harder to do.

Recently a lady pulled me aside at a conference and asked me a question that I found to be quite funny. She said, "What if I just *listen* to gossip, but I never tell another soul?" My response may not have been humorous to her but the look on her face made me smile. I responded, "Then you have sin-filled ears and they might just fall off." Of course, I was kidding, but the point I was making is it's just as wrong to listen, as it is to spread it!

There is a line I have begun to say when someone wants to gossip to me. It is comical, but gets the point across in a kind but firm way. Feel free to borrow it. I say something like, "I really like you and I like spending time with you, but I am worried that God may cut my tongue out and use it to spank my behind if I participate in gossip. I like my tongue. It's a pretty tongue. Want to see?" At first they will look stunned and then they will begin to laugh. The great part is, you have gotten the point across and they usually apologize. I guarantee you have left something for them to think about the next time they begin to gossip.

But what about the times that we are talking about others because we are **truly** concerned and want to help? How do I know the difference between gossiping and concern? Here is the difference. When we talk with someone who can do something about the problem, we are talking out of concern, not gossiping.

Using our tongue to enhance the lives of others is crucial as a follower of Jesus. Remember the Bible warns that if something offends, we have to cut it off. We need that tongue since we love to talk, so from one friend to another, *use it wisely!*

Reflection

1. Have you been the victim of gossip? How did it make you feel?

2. What will you do the next time someone approaches you with gossip? How will you know the difference between gossip and concern for another?

3. The next time you are tempted to gossip, discover the reason behind your need to so do. Are you feeling left out, alone, or unimportant? Search for ways to fill your life with God's goodness and avoid the gossiping tongue.

CHAPTER NINETEEN

Hearing from God

"My soul, wait in silence for God alone, for my expectation is from Him." Psalm 62:5 (NIV)

I had the wonderful privilege of singing *"The Star-Spangled Banner"* for a professional NFL football game one season. Practicing on the field before anyone entered the stadium was one of the most amazing moments I have ever experienced. As I walked down the tunnel and onto the field, there was silence. The only noise that could be heard from the stands was the maintenance crew doing last minute work in preparation for the 70,000 enthusiastic fans that would soon enter the stadium. I stood on the field and looked around; enjoying the unusual view I had from the 50-yard line.

When it was time to sing, I re-entered the field and saw a much different picture. Hundreds of onlookers stood on the sidelines watching the football team finish their warm ups. The bodyguard that was assigned to me never left my side as she pulled me every which way but loose to be sure that I was not lost in the crowd. Once we arrived in the middle of the field, people began screaming and waving from the stands. The media yelled, "Smile" as they took pictures and the band across the field played loudly as fans cheered. The team was introduced as their mascot went roaring in front of me on a four-wheeler, and a cannon was ignited after the introductions were made. It was so crowded on the sidelines that I almost hit the head coach in the side of the head when I tossed my throat spray back to my bodyguard. *It was sheer pandemonium.* I tried to stay focused, but it was hard to not get caught up in the excitement.

The time finally came for me to sing. After the announcer introduced me, I turned my attention to the field director. I was to follow her directions explicitly and not to begin singing one second before she gave me the cue. A fly-over was scheduled to cross the stadium as soon as I hit the last note and the timing had to be perfect.

The announcer introduced me and the crowd grew silent. I focused intently on the director and waited for my cue. She raised her hand for me to begin singing, so I put the microphone to my mouth. Immediately, the field director jumped off the turf and waved her arm in a "no" position. I lowered the microphone. As soon as I lowered the microphone, she said, "Go!" I raised it again; only to be told a second time, "Wait!" I lowered the microphone. "Go!" she signaled again, and I raised the microphone to my mouth and sang with all my heart. As I hit the last note, I heard the fly-over. As a result of everyone in the control room and aircraft working together, the crowd erupted and everything ended on a wonderful note. I still chuckle each time I watch the video of the beginning of that song.

Silence is a very important part of life. If I had begun singing when the field director instructed me to be silent, the timing of the song and fly-over would have been unsuccessful. Silence is a skill that we must learn in order to have successful communication skills. Unfortunately, it is not always one that comes easy. One of the most powerful places we can experience the rewards of silence is in our prayer time.

For years, I acted as if God were some type of Santa Claus who lived to do things my way and on my timetable. I would get frustrated when he didn't "come through," then pray harder so that I would be more effective. Once I realized that God would never be interested in working off my agenda, I stopped talking so much. I began to *listen more intently* to what He had to say so I could understand His agenda.

Why is it so difficult for us to be quiet during our prayer time? One reason is our inability to be still. We are a culture of instant everything and if God doesn't speak in two minutes, we are on to the next thing. He will have to catch us during part of our day because we are constantly on the move.

We are also uncomfortable with quiet. We live in the most technologically advanced era in history. There are few evenings spent by the fire reading a book these days. We have grown accustomed to noise and we expect God to fit in with our culture. Unfortunately, God does not always come with a shout, but in a "still, small voice." We must be listening–*quietly*–so that we don't miss him.

Fear can also cause us to speak more than we listen. Perhaps we are afraid of what we will hear God say, so we refuse to be quiet and hear the truth. The problem is we cannot have a relationship with someone when we do all the talking. This is a "one-sided" relationship and we miss out on hearing God's voice.

How can we adopt quietness and gentleness into our prayer time? First, we must relax and clear our minds of all distraction. When we do this, we become calmer and open to hearing the voice of God.

Secondly, find the setting that is right for you. Some of us concentrate better with complete silence, while others find it easier to be still with music or the constant hum of a fan in the background. Whatever sound you need to help you hear God's voice, be open to the experience.

We must also adjust our attitude toward our "quiet time." As with any relationship, listening is a skill. We must recognize that when we tell God we are listening, we are showing Him the respect and honor He deserves. Listening to Him communicates that we value what He has to say and that we respect Him as our guide.

Silence during our prayer time allows God to reveal His will to us about certain situations. We allow Him to place thoughts in our minds. Then, we can pray to understand what we need to do about the things He reveals to us.

When we are quiet, we can release the fears, anxieties and concerns that we have and hear what He wants to say about our circumstance. When we hear His voice, we hear the truth about the situation causing us concern.

"Very early in the morning, while it was still dark, Jesus got up, left the house and went off to a solitary place, where he prayed." Mark 1:35 (NIV)

A "quiet time" with God is also a time of restoration. We are so busy that we often feel like we can't take the time to sit and pray–or listen. These are the times that we need a "quiet time" the most. In Mark, we see Jesus seeking a place to be alone and to pray. Why? Because He knew that prayer was His "life line" to His Father. It is the same for us. When we don't take time to pray, we become irritable, angry, and upset. If we continue in this state, we become useless for God's Kingdom.

Today, set aside some time to spend with your Father. He loves you so much and *craves* a time to sit and talk with you. Yes, He wants to hear what is on your heart, but He also wants to share what is on His heart. Isn't that amazing? The same God who made this universe is just waiting to have some time to talk—to you!

Silence is golden. Whether it's football games or faith, it is a must if we are to have victory in our lives.

Reflection

1. Notice that Jesus was "seeking" a place of solitude. What do you need to do to make sure a place of solitude is available to you on a daily basis?
2. Is there anything keeping you from having a daily "quiet time?" Examine your priorities and rearrange something so that a time alone with God is possible.
3. What does actively listening during your "quiet time" mean to you?

CHAPTER TWENTY

Careful What You Chew On

"He who guards his mouth and his tongue, guards his soul from troubles." Proverbs 21:23 (NASB)

My husband, David, likes to play jokes on me. He often tells me things just to get a reaction out of me so the morning he woke me up to tell me I needed to go outside and look at my car, I rolled over and went back to sleep. When he came in a second time, I knew there might be some validity to his concern. I pulled myself out of bed, put my robe on and strolled out to look at my car. NOTHING.

I was somewhat irritated that I had been disturbed from a beautiful morning of sleep to look at nothing! Suddenly, he pointed to the hood. There were what seemed to be large "tongue" marks across the hood of my car. As I looked closer, however, I noticed that there were also large teeth marks! My horse had found the hood of my car to be quite tasty overnight and used it as a giant salt lick. Since that seemed to be satisfying, he obviously decided to use it as a chew toy!

My reaction to this event was surprising to both my husband and myself. I took one look at the hood, then at my husband, shrugged my shoulders and said, "I don't even know what to say." With that, I turned around, walked inside and crawled back into bed. As I lay there trying to go back to sleep, I began to chuckle. Of all of the things that have happened at the Perry home, this was one of the more bizarre. I pondered several ways of telling the auto body shop about this one before drifting back to sleep. Four hundred dollars later, we removed his chew toy from licking distance.

Just as my horse's tongue caused a great deal of damage, so can our tongue when we use it to "bite" other people. Have you looked at your tongue lately? If not, take a minute to stand in front of the mirror and stick out your tongue. Can you believe that little thing can be so powerful? With this one little muscle we have the power to enhance or destroy the lives of those we love. But don't take my word for it. God's Word has a great deal to say about the tongue.

Proverbs 6:16-19 says that there are some things about the tongue that God hates. While hate is a strong word, God must feel strongly about a lying tongue, a false witness and a man who stirs up dissension among others. According to these verses, He *really* hates when people cause dissension. So why do people do it? Most of the time, it is all they have ever known. They have grown up in an environment where dissension was the norm, and they don't know any differently.

Have you ever met someone who is divisive? They are not difficult to spot. Maybe you have even received a phone call from "Ms. Divisive." As soon as you pick up the phone, she begins telling you something about a person that you really like. Sometimes we pay it no attention. Sometimes, we begin to question our own opinions about that person, and by the time we hang up, we have "curious" feelings about that person we really liked before we answered the call. That is an act of dissension. As followers of Christ, we are to remove ourselves from things that God hates and according to Proverbs, this includes divisive acts with the tongue.

How can we avoid using our tongues in a divisive way? I have found the best way to stop divisiveness is to be grateful. There is something about using our tongue to speak words of gratitude that changes our perspective and takes us to a place of peace. The next time you are in a conversation where someone is speaking negatively about a person, challenge him or her to find something positive about that person. Just try it! When we have an "attitude of gratitude," our perspective shifts, and our divisive thoughts shift to praising God instead. It's all in what we decide to "chew" on.

Speaking of chewing and being grateful, I am thankful for the 1000-pound horse that gives me great enjoyment each time I ride him. But I will continue working with him about that tongue!

Reflection

1. Have you been the recipient or the giver of divisive acts? What have you done to remove dissension from your life?

2. What are some things that you are grateful for today? Make a list and post it where you can see it.

3. How will you respond the next time you are confronted with divisiveness?

CHAPTER TWENTY-ONE

Jesus On My Street

"We all stumble in many ways. Anyone who is never at fault in what they say is perfect, able to keep their whole body in check. When we put bits into the mouths of horses to make them obey us, we can turn the whole animal." James 3:2-3 (NIV)

A little girl was helping her mother get the table ready for dinner. A large group of church members were scheduled to arrive in the next half hour, and dinner was taking much longer to cook than expected. The little girl's mother was extremely stressed and was quite frustrated before the church members arrived. When the group finally arrived and they were seated at the table ready to eat, the little girl's mother asked her to say the blessing. "But I don't know what to say," the child responded. "Just say what mommy would say," the mother retorted. The little girl put her hands together, bowed her head, and slowly prayed, "Dear Lord, why did I invite all of these people over for dinner?"

The complaining tongue—don't you just dread conversations with these people? You know the ones I am talking about. You ask how they are doing and before you know it, you hear about everything from the sore on their toe to the bump on their behind. Soon you wonder, "Why did I even ask?"

Psalm 142:2 is a great reminder of what we should do when we feel like whining. *"I pour out my complaint before Him; before Him I tell my trouble." (NIV)* The secret to dealing with our complaints is taking them to the One who can really do something about them.

Not long ago I did a great deal of complaining about the drivers who speed up and down the street where I live. I complained to our secretary, to my husband, to my neighbors and even to the police, but no one seemed to do anything. We live in the country so the teens like to use our street as a drag strip. More than once I have been called outside at two o'clock in the morning to find a teenager's car perched on top of the culvert in our ditch. Worried that someone was going to get seriously hurt, I began to pray that God would handle this situation. What a novel idea! Why is it that we sometimes make prayer our last resort?

As I began praying, the speeding didn't stop but something miraculous happened. Jesus appeared at the end of my street! LITERALLY! I turned onto my street after a long road trip one evening and there was a ten-foot billboard of Jesus with His arms outstretched perched at the end of the road. Just like that, He showed up! I got so tickled I almost ran into Jesus. I thought of the drunk drivers who often speed down our street, and what might run through their mind when out of nowhere, Jesus appears. THAT should get their attention.

A legitimate complaint can only be resolved when we take it to the person who can change our situation. If we take our complaint to someone who can do nothing about it we need to ask ourselves this question, "Am I complaining to get sympathy or do I want a solution?"

Now we have all been in a place where we needed someone who would listen to us. When we find others who are great at feeling sorry for us but offer no suggestions for helping us move forward, they are called enablers. In other words, they help us stay right where we are–in the very place that we are complaining about. The next time you are in need of a complaining session, find someone who will sympathize with your situation, then propel you past your problem. If they don't have the answer, they will encourage you to find a source that can help. One complaint breeds another complaint; therefore, if your friend joins your complaining but offers no solutions, a healthier alternative is available.

First of all, *pray and ask God what He would have you do.* It may be that there is no need to involve another in your dilemma. If there is, ask Him to send someone who will help you find the purpose of what He wants to accomplish through your problem. Then, *take action.* Self-pity wastes time and keeps us from God's best. If the solution does not come right away, continue to seek God until you find the answer. As you seek the solution, *keep a "Gratitude List."* Find the things that you are grateful for and make a list. Complaining and being gracious is like bending over and standing up at the same time. It is impossible. When you are tempted to complain, focus on the good things that God has done. Before you know it, you will see Jesus everywhere. You may even see Him at the end of **your** street!

Reflection

1. What are some complaints you have had lately?

2. Are you taking your complaints to someone who has the authority to do something about them? If not, how will you change that?

3. Where can you see Jesus today? Keep a list of all the ways you see Jesus in your life.

Section IV

Walk a Mile in

My Shoes

"Earth's crammed with heaven,
And every common bush afire with God:
But only he who sees takes off his shoes."
- Elizabeth Barrett Browning -

"The Real Thing"

From the CD "The Real Thing"
© 2009 Paul Marino and Shannon Perry

I can convince everyone around me
how much I love you.
I can sing your praise or one of those clichés
And make them believe it's true.
But you know who I am,
and you know my heart
So take it, I don't want to fake it.

I want to be the real thing
who loves you more than anything
I want to be so genuine
When somebody's looking in my heart,
They see the real thing.

I can pretend you're my one and only, everything I
need.
I can sing your praise, with my hands upraised
So everyone knows I'm free.
But you know who I am,
and you know my heart
Lord take it, I don't want to fake it.

I want to be the real thing
who loves you more than anything
I want to be so genuine
When somebody's looking in my heart,
They see the real thing.

SHANNON PERRY

CHAPTER TWENTY-TWO

Oooh That Smell

"If we confess our sins He is faithful and just and will forgive us our sins and purify us from all unrighteousness." 1 John 1:9 (NIV)

In the last two weeks I have been in four different airports, a recording studio, done a television show, been on vacation with my husband and spoken at three different venues. Knowing some of your schedules, that is a walk in the park compared to all you do, but for me, it was quite a stretch.

I also teach voice lessons. I have many students who are very accomplished and I am honored to work with them. Recently, I had the privilege of flying to Nashville with one of my students after being hired to work with her in the studio.

Now in case you have not flown lately, an elaborate meal is no longer served aboard the airlines. On the flight to Nashville, I thought I was receiving preferred treatment when I received a turkey sandwich, carrots and some cookies. Not many airlines do that these days, so it was a nice surprise. As I began eating the sandwich, I remembered that I had no car once I got to Nashville. The young lady I was with had rented the car, so I would be in Nashville with no wheels of my own. I was unfamiliar with the hotel where we

149

would be staying, and I was unsure about restaurants nearby. Realizing this could be my last meal of the day if there were no restaurants within walking distance of my hotel, I asked the stewardess for another sandwich. She politely obliged, and I tucked the turkey sandwich neatly in the outside pocket of my purse and prepared for landing. Fortunately, Panera Bread was across from my hotel and I had a lovely time in Nashville.

Several weeks later, I was in a restaurant with my husband when suddenly a very foul smell came from my waiter. As the waiter stood close to me, all I could think was, "Bless his heart. Has anyone told him he has this problem?" Upon leaving the restaurant, we also left the smell, *or so I thought.* The next morning when I opened my closet, the smell almost knocked me over. I tore my closet apart looking for anything I could find and there was nothing. Suddenly, I began to get a complex. The smell was not coming from the waiter last evening, it was coming from me! I went to my husband and asked, "Do I stink?" With a puzzled look on his face he replied, "I don't *think* so."

Later that day I got in my car to drive to a luncheon, and the smell was with me again. *It had to be me.* I considered a doctor visit after my meeting because obviously something was terribly wrong. Upon arriving at the luncheon, one of my friends wanted to hug me. Somewhat tentative, I hugged her then quickly looked at her face for any signs of disapproval. I didn't see any, but she was also in full time ministry so I assumed she had been trained for moments like these.

As we sat at our table all I could think about was "the stink." We finally finished our luncheon and it was time to pay the bill. I reached into the outside pocket of my purse to retrieve my cash when I suddenly hit something squishy at the bottom. As I pulled my hand from the pocket, I thought I would pass out from the smell – it was THE SANDWICH! For three weeks I had carried that turkey sandwich in hot cars, airplanes and hotels without realizing it. Relieved that it was not emanating from my body, I thrust my hand into the air and screamed, "It's not me!" My luncheon guest smiled a very curious smile, so I told her the story. After laughing until our sides hurt, I pulled the sandwich from my purse. Unrecognizable at this point, the waitress quickly picked it up and discarded it. My purse went to be with Jesus and, from now on, I will take my chances on finding food to eat when I am out of town!

Have you ever had something that "stinks" in your life? Sin often causes our lives to smell. Just as I needed to take the time to clean my purse, as Christians we must take the time to clean out our lives. When we begin to walk in disobedience to God's Word, our lives can begin to smell. Unfortunately, we often try to cover the sin instead of address it. This only makes us smell worse.

SHANNON PERRY

Take your refrigerator for example. If something
inside the refrigerator smells, you can spray it with air
freshener, open a box of baking soda or just slam the
refrigerator door shut. The problem is, the smell will
still be there the next time you open the refrigerator,
and it will most likely smell worse. Why? *Because you
have not removed the source of the smell.*

When sin causes our lives to "stink" we have to
remove the source of the smell. Although sin sepa-
rates us from our Heavenly Father, God is not out to
beat us over the head by convicting of us sin. He
exposes the "smell" of sin in our lives because He
wants nothing to stand between Him and us.

So how do we get rid of the "stink?" Simple.

Pray Psalm 139: 23-24:
*Search me, O God, and know my heart; test me and
know my anxious thoughts. See if there is any
offensive way in me, and lead me in the way everlasting. (NIV)*

When we ask God to forgive us, we turn away from
the source of the smell. We get rid of whatever is
causing our lives to stink, and we don't put it back in
our lives. If it creeps back in, it is because we have
left an opening for it to come back and "stink the
place up" again.

Obedience is key when we long to walk in fellowship
with Jesus. If God's Word has shown you something
as sin, remove it from your life-immediately! Get the

"stink" out and allow the beautiful aroma of God's presence to permeate every area of your life today.

Reflection

1. If you were having lunch with God, is there any sin in your life that might "stink" to Him?

2. What do you need to do to get rid of the sin that is "stinking up" that part of your life?

3. Who will you ask to hold you accountable to help make sure that you keep the "smell" of sin out of your life?

CHAPTER TWENTY-THREE

Love Ruts

"And now these three remain: faith, hope and love.
But the greatest of these is love."
1 Corinthians 13:13 (NIV)

On February 14, 1993, I was asked to sing at my first wedding. It was the second marriage for both the bride and groom, and the ceremony was to be held in the bride's home. Having never sung at a wedding before, I charged them a whopping thirty dollars to sing two songs. If you have had the privilege of hosting a wedding lately, you know thirty dollars is quite a bargain. The bride and groom got a deal, and I was grateful for the opportunity.

Three days before the wedding was to take place, my duet partner called to let me know he would not be able to sing. I tried desperately to contact the bride and let her know we would need to choose another song, but I was unable to reach her. The day of the wedding, I nervously approached her and let her know that I would not be able to sing one of the two songs she had requested. After breaking into tears, she let me know that I would need to learn another song.

That's when the "fun" began.

Two minutes before the procession, I wrote the words to the new song she requested, and pinned them to the back of a chair. I sang to the best of my ability as she descended the staircase to meet her groom and two hundred guests. After the wedding was over, I quickly got my thirty dollars and headed toward my car. I longed to leave this experience "at the altar."

While walking to the car with my date, we suddenly discovered that the two hundred guests were parked behind us. We were blocked in. Desperate to avoid interruption, we devised a plan. If we could drive through the bride's front yard, we could escape without bothering anyone.

We cautiously proceeded through the yard. As we passed the long column windows where the guests were seated having dinner, they looked on in disbelief. We thought we had made our escape until suddenly, our worst fears became reality. We were stuck in the bride's front yard.

The wedding guests got up from dinner to move their cars so a groomsman could pull us out of the mud with his truck. After he also got stuck, more guests came to move their cars to make room for the tow truck that would now pull both of us from the mud. After paying the tow truck driver seventy-five dollars, I was officially forty-five dollars "in the hole" as a wedding singer.

As the tow truck removed my car, two large, wet, muddy ruts were left in the ground. "Great," I thought. Now the bride and groom would have a reminder forever "etched" in their front yard to remind them of my participation in the wedding.

I offered to pay for the damages left by our "plan of escape." To my surprise, the bride and groom began laughing, telling me how much entertainment I had been for the guests. The bride even apologized for being so harsh about the song, claiming she had forgotten to call me back during the midst of all the wedding chaos. I thanked them for their graciousness, and used the driveway this time as my means of escape.

This bride and groom were a shining example of 1 Corinthians 13. They chose to react with love and kindness. Kenneth S. Wuest, who brings out the meaning of each Greek word in 1 Corinthians 13: 4-8, translates this scripture the following way:

> *"Love meekly and patiently bears ill treatment from others. Love is kind, gentle, benign, pervading and penetrates the whole nature. Love does not brag, nor does it show itself off…love believes all things, hopes all things, bears up under all things, not losing heart nor courage. Love never fails."*

Perhaps you would like to leave more favorable "ruts" on the hearts of the ones you love. Make 1 Corinthians 13 a verb in your life. Gifts are easy to buy. Giving of ourselves sacrificially and unselfishly costs us something. What action can you perform that will leave a lasting impression, or "rut," on your loved one's heart? Get creative. Do something DRASTIC! Leave a "rut" that is such an amazing demonstration of love it will last for years to come, and when they look back, they will know you were there.

Jesus, you left an indelible "rut" on our lives when you gave up your life on the cross. Because of your death and resurrection, we have the power to love others outrageously. Help me to leave lasting "ruts" of 1 Corinthians 13 on the lives of all I meet.

Reflection

1. What acts of love have left "ruts" on your heart?

2. What acts of love have you demonstrated that have left "ruts" on the hearts of others?

3. What can you do to leave a "love rut" on the life of someone you encounter today?

CHAPTER TWENTY-FOUR

Get Under the Umbrella

"And we know that for those who love God all things work together for good, for those who are called according to his purpose." Romans 8:28 (NIV)

As a former schoolteacher and school counselor, I have many wonderful memories of the first day of school. One particular scenario that brings a smile to my face is the kindergartner who stopped me in the hallway on his first day. Carrying a backpack longer than his body, he tapped me on the arm, reached up and whispered, "I am not sure that I have the right teacher." I smiled as he told me why. "My mom said that teachers are only nice after Christmas, but my teacher is smiling and it's only August."

Just like this little boy, I have often believed that I might have the "wrong" thing in my life when what I have been told does not match with what I can see. I often question God just as the little boy questioned me. One such time came on the first day of my last year in Education. I had new clothes, new make up, new Day-Timer pages and a clean desk. I also had a new year in which I could start each day with prayer. This New Year would be no exception. I read my Bible, prayed, and asked God for help to be the best school counselor that any Christian can be in the public school setting. After my prayer, I grabbed my briefcase and headed for the car.

The first day of school usually brought a spring to my step as I anticipated the adventures of a new year. This morning, however, seemed different. As I pulled out of the driveway and headed toward the school, I clearly heard God speak. *"You are not to go back to school this year."* Immediately, I began to laugh. After all, there were bills to be paid and being newly married I had to let my husband know that I would carry my end of the weight. Perhaps this was just my head reminding me that there would be no more days of "freedom" until next June.

When I arrived at school, I felt a heaviness and lack of enthusiasm. Believing that I must be tired from preparing for the new school year, I trudged on and greeted the children with a smile. As the days rolled into months, however, my heaviness became greater and so did the problems that I faced on my job.

One particular school day stands out. I arrived at my office at the usual time. I had not even unlocked my office door when our school secretary approached me. "Shannon, there has been a murder. The parents of two of our students have been killed, and we need you to verify that CPS has the children in custody." Suddenly I went from greeting children in the hallway to needing a badge and a gun! I drove to the murder scene and made sure that our children were safe. As I left the scene, I specifically remember almost running over the blue coroner's glove lying on the sidewalk.

"Just another day at the office," I thought. Many would be shocked at the things Educators deal with on a "typical" day.

Upon arriving back to school from the murder scene, I answered the phone to yet another emergency. A hysterical mother claimed that her ex-husband had kidnapped her daughter and needed me to help her find her child. I talked her through the hysteria so we could get to a place of reason, and then turned it over to the authorities. "Surely this is the end of crazy for one day," I thought.

Moments after handling that phone call the school secretary was back at my office door. "Shannon, we need you to go to the gym immediately. There is a dad in there that is angry that his child was accidentally hit in the eye by a jump rope yesterday. He has our principal pinned against the wall swinging a jump rope at her, and he has destroyed the gym. The children have been removed, but we need you to stand in there with her until the police arrive."

Now, I know what you must be thinking by now, *"What kind of school is this?"* It actually is a very nice school district, but undoubtedly, several of our families were having a **very** bad day.

After my more than exhausting day, I went home, flopped on the couch and tried to forget the events of the day. I was able to keep my composure until my husband came home, looked at me and said, "I have had a very bad day." He then went on to tell me about his "very bad day." Stewing as I listened to what seemed to be a walk in the park compared to my day, I responded in a harsh tone of voice, "*You* had a bad day? Let me tell you about *my* day!" I went on to tell him about the events of my day when suddenly he looked at me with a calm demeanor, pointed his finger and said, "And you're done."

Just like that, my world went from murder scenes and hysterical moms to fourteen years of a career crashing to a screeching halt. My husband insisted I quit my job and I was to do so immediately.

Thinking about the decision before me, I was suddenly reminded of what God had whispered on that first day of school. *"You are not to go back to school this year."* God did not mean, "Only if you feel like it." His command had been very clear and I had disobeyed. As a result, I walked out from underneath the umbrella of His grace and protection and faced some very difficult obstacles as a result.

The following day, I walked into my principal's office and explained my need to resign. During this time my dad was also having heart problems and I needed to be there for my family. There were many reasons I needed to resign, but not one that was appropriate according to district guidelines. I expected great resistance from my principal, but what I got was a beautiful surprise. My Christian principal said through tears, "Shannon, I believe God has great things planned for your life. We actually had you longer than I expected. We will miss you terribly, but I know that God has plans to use your gifts and talents in a powerful way." Just like that, I had been given the grace to do what God had told me to do in the first place.

After cleaning out my office I went home and sat at the end of the bed. I cried and asked God to forgive me for being disobedient, then held my hands up in the air and asked, *"Now what?"* I would love to say He gave me the answer right away, but instead I spent the next five years of my life muddling through what He would have me do. In those five years, He shaped the beautiful ministry that I have the privilege of taking part in today.

Many times we try to do things out of God's grace and timing, and it simply doesn't work. Just like the little boy thought he might have the wrong teacher when what he heard and saw did not match, we often believe what we hear and see must match before we can take a step. In God's "line of work" however, it does not happen that way. The opposite is often the case.

When we hear the voice of God it is sometimes months or even years until we see the plan unfold. That is what faith is all about. *We are to move when God says move even when the circumstances don't appear to match what we are hearing.* In order to walk in God's grace, we must walk under His umbrella of guidance. It may not always be easy, but there will be a peace that comes as a result. It is when we get out from underneath the umbrella of God's grace and protection that we get ourselves into trouble. If we are behind or ahead, we are not covered, and we are left in the most frightening position—away from God.

In Luke 2:41-52, Mary and Joseph made plans to return to their hometown of Nazareth after enjoying the Feast of the Passover in Jerusalem. There was only one problem. They traveled half a day before they realized that Jesus was not with them. They had to go back and see where they had lost Him. If you are like me, many times I make my own plans, only to find myself like Mary and Joseph. Half way through my journey, I have to go back to find out where I became separated from Jesus.

Are you feeling heavy, weighed down and hopeless today? Perhaps there is a place where you walked out from underneath the umbrella of God's grace and didn't even realize it. Maybe He was saying one thing but what you could see made much more sense and you took another road. Today He is standing right where you left Him. He is holding the umbrella and waiting for you to come running back under His protection. The beautiful thing is that He never folds up His umbrella of grace. It is always open and ready to cover us no matter how long we have been away.

God can take anything and use it for His good when we are under His umbrella. God has a way of working all things for our good when we walk in the shadow of His grace, so look up precious one! Can you see the umbrella overhead?

Reflection

1. Is there an area in your life where you have walked away from God? Take a step toward Him today. He is waiting right where you left Him.

2. Do you need to take a step of faith today? Is there something that God is encouraging you to do, but it doesn't make sense? Take a step on faith and watch what He can do.

3. What are some habits you will incorporate into your life to be sure that you stay under "God's umbrella?"

CHAPTER TWENTY-FIVE

A Mother's Prayer

"Devote yourselves to prayer, being watchful and thankful." Colossians 4:2 (NIV)

My home state of Texas made national news when soldiers at Ft. Hood were viciously attacked by an imposter on their own soil. As I watched the chain of events unfold on television, I grieved deeply for the families of these brave men and women so unjustly snatched from us.

As the mother of a U.S. soldier, I felt compelled to show support for the victims. I walked to the flagpole in my front yard and silently prayed as I lowered the stars and stripes to half-mast. Little did I know that during my silent time of grieving, I received a text message that would forever impact my prayer life. It simply said, "Mom, it's hard here. Please pray for me."

The second year I taught first grade, a beautiful little six-year-old blonde-haired, blue-eyed boy wearing OshKosh B'Gosh® overalls and red tennis shoes walked into my classroom. He stuck out his hand and said, "Hi, my name is Sean." I had never seen a more beautiful child. After greeting Sean, I stood up and saw his daddy standing behind him and quickly recognized where Sean had inherited his good looks.

I also learned that his father was raising Sean alone. His mom had not been actively involved in his life since he was three.

As the school year progressed, so did my interest in Sean. I watched one of his particular habits very closely—his love for planes. Sean had a habit of forming his tiny fingers into the shape of a plane and flying them around the classroom while I was teaching. I was constantly saying, *"Sean Perry, land that plane!"* He would quickly bring his fingers in for a landing, and begin working on his assignment.

Over the years I lost contact with Sean and his father, but I often thought of them. Sean's dad had expressed interest in dating once or twice, but I refused due to "conflict of interest." Twelve years later, however, God fulfilled the desires of my heart. I was reunited with Sean and his father, and eight months later, Sean's dad and I were married. That beautiful little boy was now my son.

I had the privilege of watching Sean graduate from high school and receive a full scholarship to the sixth-ranked academic institution in the United States. The most amazing celebration came the day I watched him march onto the field of the United States Air Force Academy and graduate as a Second Lieutenant. That same little boy who had flown his fingers like a plane in my classroom would now fly planes in defense of our country.

After graduation, Sean attended flight school. It was challenging, especially in the area of landing the planes, and Sean often asked me to pray for him. On the day of the attack at Fort Hood, Sean was due to take his final flight test in Colorado. If he passed, he would fly. If he did not, he would walk away from his childhood dream. Conflicting emotions roared in me. On the same day my son was longing to defend his country, another was snatching lives of soldiers at Fort Hood.

I prayed for 24 hours straight as Sean prepared to take his test. I asked God to help Sean *"land that plane."* I had repeated this phrase many times when he was my student, but now, it had become my constant prayer as his mother. I must admit that I worked hard to keep my selfish will out of those prayers. After seeing death steal the lives of soldiers at Fort Hood, I struggled when asking God to equip my only child for battle. I had waited all these years for him, and could not imagine life without him. As I prayed, however, God quickly reminded me that Sean's life was His business, and that He would be in control. I could trust Him.

The following day, I received another text message while sitting in a local coffee shop. It simply read, "You have a divine connection. I passed my test and I will take my first solo flight next Monday. Thanks for your prayers, Mom. I love you, Sean." As any calm, rational parent would do, I began sobbing and grabbed a total stranger by the shoulders to tell them of my exciting news. *"Sean Perry landed that plane!"* God had heard my prayers, and His plan for Sean would not be thwarted.

God has exciting plans for your children too! He knew them before the foundation of the world, and His plan is *"to prosper them and not to harm them, to give them a future and a hope"* according to Jeremiah 29:11 (NIV). The Bible is full of promises for parents, and we can trust God with our children. Are you worried about your children's salvation? Pray 2 Peter 3:9 over them. God's will is that *"none should perish, but that all should come to repentance"* (NIV). Are you concerned that they will be equally yoked some day? Pray 2 Corinthians 6:14, asking God to yoke them with believers. Do you want to see your children totally surrender to God? Pray James 4:7 over them. Prayer is the most powerful weapon we have as parents.

We must daily submit our children to God. He loves them so much, and His promises stand true. We may not know what the landing will look like, but we can trust that *our children are flying with the most experienced pilot when God is in control.* Pray for your children, and then trust that God has charted the perfect course as they soar through life.

Reflection

During your prayer time, be sure to lift up your children with the following verses. If you are not a parent, pray for children in general or those that you know. Our children are under vicious attack by the enemy of our soul, and they need our prayers covering them.

- Acts 19:20–I thank you Father that Your Word prevails over my children.

- Isaiah 54:13–Great is their peace and undisturbed composure.

- 1 Peter 1:14–They are obedient, not conforming to the things of the flesh.

- 1 Peter 1:15–They are holy, in all their conduct.

- 2 Peter 3:18–They will grow in the grace and knowledge of Jesus.

- James 1:22–They are doers of the Word and not hearers only.

- 2 Timothy 1:7–They do not have a spirit of fear, but of peace, love and a sound mind.

- John 10:5–They will in no way follow strangers, not knowing their voices.

- 1 John 5:18–Jesus keeps them safe, the wicked one does not touch them.

- 1 John 2:15–They do not love the world or the things in the world.

- Proverbs 3:4–They have high esteem with God and man.

CHAPTER TWENTY-SIX

Row Three

"For who makes you different from anyone else? What do you have that you did not receive? And if you did receive it, why do you boast as though you did not?" 1 Corinthians 4:7 (NIV)

Unexpected blessings still amaze me. When God blesses me through the giving of others, I occasionally struggle with receiving the gift because I have done nothing to "earn" it. I am slowly learning to smile and say, "Thank you Lord," when unexpected blessings occur. I know God will bless someone else as a result of my blessings. One such blessing is forever etched in my memory.

After being asked to appear on a popular Christian television show, I packed up my mom and we flew to Chicago. I thought it would be nice to spend some mother/daughter time together. After arriving in Chicago, we drove to Indiana where the show would be taped and enjoyed some sightseeing.

The next morning, we woke up at 4:30 a.m. to prepare for the show. While my mother likes to be an hour early to everything, I prefer to pull into the parking lot and "get the show on the road." We were early that morning–an hour to be exact.

As we talked while waiting in the parking lot, I told my mom how guilty I felt for taking this trip. She was shocked so I explained. I was struggling with spending the five hundred dollars that it cost to fly to Chicago. I tried to be very diligent with the ministry's money and there was no income on this trip. I felt God leading me to do the television show, however, so I made the arrangements. She helped soothe my conscious by sharing that she viewed the trip as a vacation with me. We did not do a lot of long distance traveling when I was younger, so the money I was spending was worth the memories we were making. I felt somewhat better.

The show went great as we talked at length about writing the music and topics for *If the Shoe Fits* while David was undergoing radiation treatment. We talked a great deal about how God healed David's cancer and I closed by singing "Keep On Pressing On." Emails and phone calls came in as a result of the show, and many were blessed by the message and music.

After the interview, mom and I departed Indiana and returned to Chicago. We saw amazing things in downtown Chicago, and made our last stop at the seven-story Macy's department store. We had lunch on the seventh floor, and spent an hour gawking at all the goodies that would never fit into our suitcases. After this wonderful, whirlwind day, we headed for the airport exhausted and ready to get home. We were looking forward to a nice relaxing plane ride until we arrived at the airport and discovered our plane had been delayed for three hours!

After hours of phones ringing and babies screaming, we were finally cleared for boarding. The airline we were flying makes you board by groups since there are no assigned seats. Like cattle, we found our "post" and were greeted by one who was not happy that we were part of "her" group. "Miss Thing" quickly let my mom know that she and her husband were "in line first" and went on to remind mom that we "would be boarding behind" her and her husband. Fortunately, God either allowed me to go deaf for those few minutes or I was so tired, I was not aware that my mother was being unjustly scolded. Had I heard her, "Miss Thing" may have heard more out of me than scripture.

As we prepared to board, the child in front of us wailed louder than Pavarotti. Children's toys and pacifiers flew past my face, and "Miss Thing" informed all of us that Side A would board before Side B. The man behind me pushed his luggage over my foot, which caused my initial thoughts to suddenly reoccur: *I spent five hundred dollars for this!*

Once aboard the aircraft, "Mister and Miss Thing" decided to stop and have a conversation at the third row of seats. Since a 737 has many options from which to choose, I stood patiently waiting for a decision to be made. They did not make a decision quickly, and their conversation suddenly turned into an argument. While "Miss Thing" wanted to sit in the third row because she would be one of the first to get off the plane once it landed, "Mister Thing" preferred to sit further back. My lessons in "Lacing Up the Tongue" went right out the window. Standing directly behind "Mister Thing" I blurted, "Let's not make a career out of it. Either sit down or move on." "Mister Thing" got his way and down the row they went. I prayed for Jesus to forgive me, then quickly sat down in row three and pulled my mom in beside me.

Exhausted after the day in Chicago, I prepared for a wonderful nap on the plane ride home. Just as I was getting comfortable, I heard God whisper, *"Say hello to the man seated next to you."* I was hoping I misunderstood. From television shows to traveling with "Miss Thing," I had earned the right to nap! Surely God would want me to minister when I was more "fresh" and felt more "anointed." Wrong again. The next thing I heard was, *"Say hello."*

As you know, God is kind but relentless when He has a plan that He needs executed. I knew if I didn't do what He was telling me to do, I wouldn't sleep anyway. With a half-hearted voice, I looked over at the man next to the window and said, "Hello." He said, "Hello." That was the end of it. Feeling obedient, I prepared to sleep. Just as I leaned back to close my eyes, the man asked me, "So are you here on business?" *This was it.* I know once I start talking with someone on a flight it is always awkward to try to end the conversation because they are right there.

I answered politely, "Business. And you?" The man explained how he was in Chicago on business but this plane ride was an emergency trip home. With that statement, huge tears began falling out of his eyes. He went on to tell me that his wife had called him that day with the doctor's news. They found a mass and they are very concerned. I listened for the next twenty minutes as he poured out love and concern for his wife. After he was done, I asked, "May I tell you why I was in Chicago today?"

I told him about the television interview. I told him how God had given David and me a testimony of His grace during that very dark time in our lives. I then told him how I had written the music and messages of **If the Shoe Fits**. At this point the man began to sob. Through tears and barely able to speak he said, *"God put you next to me on this flight!"* I quickly thought, "Buddy if you only knew who almost sat next to you." He went on to tell me that he was a Christian and how a team of people back home had prayed for him to be surrounded with peace on his flight. He then pointed his finger at me and said, "God put you here. You are my answer to all of their prayers."

As the conversation progressed, I asked more about his wife and then asked if I could pray for her. Right there on the third row of that 737, we had church! Mom, my new friend and I held hands and thanked God for divine appointments. Then we prayed that God would bring peace to my friend and his wife, and that The Healer would hold them in the palm of His hands. At this point, the lady on the second row was craning her neck to see what was going on behind her, and the little boy who was running up and down the row stopped to stare.

My new friend asked more about my ministry, so I shared a little more and gave him a CD. I asked him to give it to his wife and have her listen to *"Keep On Pressing On."* I shared how I had sung the song on the show that day and felt sure these were just the lyrics she needed to hear. As we continued talking, my friend began to laugh and his heaviness seemed to all but disappear. God had truly placed me on row three of that plane to be a blessing to my new friend. *What I didn't know is the blessing He had in store for me.*

Halfway through our flight, my friend turned to me and asked, "How is your ministry funded?" I told him that churches compensate me for my time and that is how we have the finances to minister in different places. Suddenly, he reached into his wallet and took out a wad of money. He pulled out a one hundred dollar bill from the top of the pile and held it. Then he pulled off another, and another until he was holding FIVE one hundred dollar bills. He took my hand and said, "God wants you to have this." Immediately I was reminded of the conversation my mother and I had in the parking lot earlier that morning. Five hundred dollars! Exactly what I needed to pay for the trip! God had supplied all of my needs *"according to His glorious riches..."* *(Philippians 4:19 NIV)* and I had never been more grateful for missing a nap!

I immediately began to cry and my mother was not far behind. Row three had gone from a battleground with "Miss Thing" to Holy Ground with God. After thanking my new friend as best I could, I shared why five hundred dollars was so significant. You can imagine the smile on his face as I told him my story.

After landing, I met my friend's family and exchanged numbers so we could keep in touch. Even as I write this, they are at the doctor finding out the results of more tests. I don't know the specifics of what the future holds for that family, but I was clearly reminded on that trip of the One who holds my future. When God calls us to do something, He will always provide us with what we need. As God reminded me on that plane ride home, all we have is on loan. I did nothing to earn that five hundred dollars, but God through His faithfulness, allowed me to experience the generosity of Kingdom giving.

The next time God calls you to do something, don't be too anxious to nap. If He is asking you be the giver or receiver, there will be a blessing when He is involved. All we have is His, so *be anxious to obey*. You never know what surprises He may have in store!

Reflection

1. In what specific area do you need God to miraculously supply your needs?

2. How are you actively watching for, and recognizing, God's provision in your life?

3. Is there an area in your life where God is asking you to step out? How will you move toward what He is asking you to do even when you cannot see His provision with your natural eyes? Do you trust His provision to be there for you?

4. Find a Scripture about God's provision in your situation and repeat it aloud. Remind God that your trust is in Him.

CHAPTER TWENTY-SEVEN

It's all in A Name

"The Spirit himself testifies with our spirit that we are God's children. Now if we are children, then we are heirs—heirs of God and co-heirs with Christ, if indeed we share in his sufferings in order that we may also share in his glory." Romans 8:16-17 (NIV)

There is no question about it; I have always been a Daddy's girl. When I was little, Dad and I had a routine we followed religiously. Every night, we would fix a bowl of ice cream, pile Hershey's syrup on top, then sit and eat while we watched television. Next, my dad would talk to me about my day then rock me to sleep. I gave up the ice cream when it no longer served my figure, but I never gave up wanting my dad to rock me. There was something comforting about being in the strong arms of my father. To this day, it is not unusual for me to plop down in my Daddy's lap and give him a big hug as I tell him about all that is going on in my life.

Growing up, Dad had two nicknames for me. One was "Moose." I know, not the most endearing of names. He thought they were cute, so that's how that happened. The other was simply, "Kid." If he ever called me by my *real* name, I was usually in trouble.

This tradition of nicknames has followed me into adulthood. David calls me "Chae." If he addresses me by my real name, something is wrong. My mom always calls me "Darling," so these days, I answer to just about anything.

Recently while appearing on a live television show, the host repeatedly called me, "Sharon." Since there was a large teleprompter behind my head, I decided to have some fun. When my host, Stefan, apologized for calling me Sharon numerous times, I responded, "No problem, Stephanie." He began laughing, and so did the entire camera crew. We could laugh because we know who we really are.

The word *name* is defined as "a word or a combination of words by which a person, place, or thing, a body or class, or any object of thought is designated, called or known." (Dictionary.com) As Christians, we have been "designated" and "known" by THE King to be grafted into His family. This is not just *any* King. He is the ruler over every king who was, is and is to come. He is IT. There is no one who has ever been greater and there is no one coming who will ever be greater. You have arrived when you are a daughter of this King! And when you are His daughter it means you have a Daddy! You have His royal blood flowing through those beautiful veins of yours. And the best part is that **He chose you!** There are no stepchildren or second-class citizens in our Daddy's Kingdom. We wear His name and His name alone for our identification.

The next time that you are feeling like you don't belong, like you have been forgotten, or you are being called by a name that is not who you are, remember whose name you are wearing. The Daddy whose name is on your spiritual birth certificate can fix it if it's broken, heal it if it's hurt, correct it if it's wrong, feed it if it's hungry, pay it if it's due, find it if it's lost, and hear it when it cries. *Your Daddy can do anything!*

When our identity is hidden in Jesus, it doesn't matter what the world tries to make us believe. We are secure knowing that the name we wear is the name above ALL names, and we will forever be called His "kid."

Reflection

1. What do you do when you are inappropriately identified?

2. What Scripture can you carry with you to help remind you whose name is on your SPIRITUAL birth certificate?

3. Make a list of the things that are rightfully yours because of the name that you wear. Find Scripture that reminds you of all that is yours because of your "namesake." (Example–in Genesis, He is the Creator of everything. We have creativity flowing through us because our Father is creative).

CHAPTER TWENTY-EIGHT

Finish Strong

"Do you not know that in a race all the runners run, but only one gets the prize? Run in such a way as to get the prize." 1 Corinthians 9:24 (NIV)

Beginning a task is something that many of us enjoy. Finishing, however, can often be the challenge.

Finishing strong is a reoccurring theme throughout the Bible, and one that we must implement in our lives as Christians if we are to run the race with endurance. Just as a runner must learn how to pace themselves for long distances, we must learn how to pace ourselves when problems arise.

In John 16:33, Jesus reminds us, *"In this world you will have trouble. But take heart! I have overcome the world." (NIV)* As Christians, we have One who is "able to do exceedingly above all that we could think or ask." (Ephesians 3:20 NKJV, paraphrased) But how does that work in a practical way? How can we finish strong when we are surrounded by difficulty?

In II Timothy 4:2-10, Paul serves as a great example of finishing strong. During his last moments of life in prison, Paul writes to Timothy encouraging him to *"keep your head in all situations, endure hardship, do the work of an evangelist, discharge all the duties of your ministry." (v. 5 NIV)* Pretty amazing, isn't it? Instead of lying down in his cell to die, Paul scribbles words that would drastically impact the lives of Christians for generations. One of his greatest writings echoes from the hollow cavern of that prison cell. Paul clearly demonstrates determination to not only overcome, but also thrive in the middle of the problem. Nothing could keep him from continuing the work God called him to do, even the impending threat of death.

So how can we live like Paul during difficult times? First, *we must be willing to accept what we cannot change.* Paul was imprisoned unjustly and sentenced to die, yet he chose to focus on how he could make the most of his final moments. When we learn to accept the things that we cannot change, we allow room for God to move on our behalf. While we do what God has called us to do in the middle of the problem, we trust Him to do those things that we cannot do.

Secondly, *refuse to live in self-pity.* Self-pity denies God and puts self on the throne. In essence, self-pity says that God does not really know what he is doing, and that we know best. When we indulge in self-pity, we deny the power of God and focus only on our expectations and will. Trust is the opposite of self-pity. When we trust God, self-pity is denied because we know that God is faithful and has our best interests at heart.

We must also *learn to forgive* in order to finish strong. How many relationships are tarnished or destroyed because we insist on nursing a grudge? It is impossible to finish strong with God, others, or ourselves if we continue to hold on to the bitter root of unforgiveness.

If we are to cross the finish line and hear *"well done good and faithful servant," (Matthew 25:21 NIV)* we must trust that God is our vindicator and that He will repay for the harm done to us.

Finally, *we must be peacemakers.* Peacemakers would rather be reconciled than be right. As the curtains began to close on Paul's life, he did not focus on those who had unjustly abused and mistreated him. Instead,   he encouraged generations of those that he would never meet. Paul put his final stamp of faith on paper when he wrote, *"I have fought the good fight, I have finished the race, I have kept the faith." (2 Timothy 4:7 NIV)* From his prison cell, hidden from all humanity, comes a voice that will echo through the end of time. Paul knew how to finish strong. He treasured the crown of righteousness that was awaiting him, and did not lose his focus in the most difficult times.

So, where are you in the race? How do you plan to live so that your days, months, and years end with a strong finish? When you are tempted to give in, remember Paul and his prison cell. You may be in the midst of dark days, but hold on! Allow God to turn your "prison" into the place that you have your greatest impact.

Reflection

1. Is there something in your life you would like to change but cannot? Put the situation in God's hands and ask Him to help you understand the difference between what you can and cannot change.

2. In what area of your life is it easy to engage in self-pity? What are the advantages of self-pity? Disadvantages?

3. Do you live life so that it is more important to be reconciled than to be right? Is there someone you need to make things right with today? If so, ask God for His wisdom in handling the situation.

About the Author

Shannon **Perry** is a speaker/singer whose new *If The Shoe Fits* women's conferences combine her teaching prowess with her musical talent. Perry's new music CD "The Real Thing" (produced by LifeWay writer/producer Paul Marino) features songs specifically written to fit the theme of the conferences. Perry wrote the bulk of the original presentation in hospital waiting rooms while her husband, David, was undergoing cancer treatment.

Perry earned her Master's Degree in Education with an emphasis in counseling, and taught in the public school system over fourteen years before entering into full-time ministry. She has previously released music projects with both Daywind and Benson Records, which garnered radio airplay on the national Christian charts. She has performed with the Houston Symphony, appeared at Carnegie Hall, and has sung before 70,000 fans during a Houston Texans NFL game. She has been a featured soloist at the J&J Music Conferences in Houston, Texas, and led praise and worship at numerous women's conferences, and for the national LifeWay conferences held annually in New Mexico and North Carolina.

Perry is a contributing writer for *Crosswalk.com*, one of the largest Christian websites in the world with over 24 million page views per month. She has contributed articles to various publications including *Christian Voice Magazine*, *Christian Women of Today*, among others.   Shannon hosts her own talk show on *Blog-TalkRadio.com* and is currently working on a television pilot.

For more information, visit
www.ShannonPerry.com.

More Inspirational Resources from Shannon Perry

Available MUSIC CD's

"The Real Thing" includes songs written especially for each topic of *If the Shoe Fits*. Co-written with LifeWay writer/producer Paul Marino. Songs like *"Bad Hair Day"* and *"Keep On Pressing On"* garnered nationwide attention on radio. The song *"Long Way Home"* was written especially for Shannon's son Sean who serves in the United States Air Force.

Shannon's third CD, **"Tell the Story"** includes incredible music played by Grammy award winning musicians as well as songs that hit the national radio charts. Songs include *"Who's Gonna Love Me, God Is Doing Great Things, Tell the Story,"* and a song that Shannon sings especially for her dad entitled *"Love Never Ends."*

"Safe Place" is Shannon's sophomore project and includes seven original songs penned by Shannon including, *"David's*

Song," written for her husband, and *"Safe Place,"* one of the most requested songs that Shannon sings.

"Reflections," Shannon's freshman project, is a great variety of Southern Gospel and Light Contemporary. Songs like, *"Keep Walking On"* and *"Holy Ground"* are sure to lift your heart as you listen. Shannon sings, *"Thanks Again"* in honor of her mom and dad.

Available in AUDIO CD and DVD format from the teaching series *If the Shoe Fits*

"Goody Two Shoes" emphasizes the importance of balance and knowing our purpose. Jesus never had a Franklin Planner or a Blackberry, yet He lived the most balanced life of any man who ever walked the face of the earth. Through humor and scripture, Shannon reminds us that we will live balanced lives when we know our purpose.

In **"Lacing Up the Tongue,"** Shannon uses the practical illustration of a bridle along with scripture to remind us how we can heal or hurt those that we love the most by the words we speak. This session looks at the different tongues we want to avoid if we are to tame our tongue for God's glory.

 Shannon shows us what scripture teaches about the promise of God's healing when we have been hurt in **"Is There a Hole in Your Sole."** Find out how to move forward into the amazing plans God has for us when we allow Him to have full control of the circumstances that hold us captive.

 Holiness—we hear it often in church, but what does Holiness look like in today's world? In the session **"Walk A Mile In My Shoes,"** Shannon reminds us that there are practical ways that we can live Holy lives, and reminds us of the blessings we will incur when we "walk a mile in HIS shoes."

To order these available resources,
visit the "Store" at www.ShannonPerry.com.

You may also contact us at
Chae Music—281-304-1278,
or send email to
sales@shannonperry.com.

Notes

Notes

Notes

Notes

Notes

Notes

Notes

SHANNON PERRY

Notes

SHANNON PERRY

Notes

We want to hear from you! Please visit
Amazon.com and other on-line retailers to
write a customer review about

Grace in High Heels